Louis Stettner

Introduction by Virginie Chardin

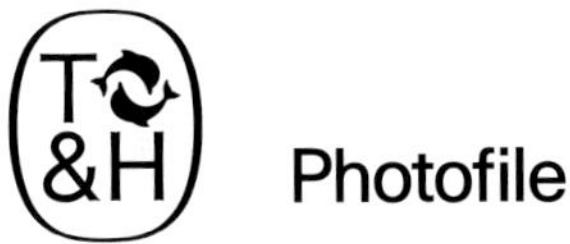

Photofile

The Man Rather Than the Incident

From the moment the creative photographer picks up his camera, he is entering into a new relationship with the world around him. Henceforth, nothing will be commonplace or taken for granted. He becomes dedicated to finding what is meaningful beneath surface reality and searching for what lies beyond the facade of appearances.[1]

Since the early 2000s, several major retrospectives have allowed the work of Louis Stettner to be viewed in all its complexity. Nevertheless his images, impossible to pin down to a particular time period or movement, continue to evade attempts at easy classification. They retain their mystery and sometimes their strangeness. Throughout his life, however, the artist himself clearly explained his philosophy and creative vision, which changed very little from his youth onward.

Learning from the Photo League · In 1946, sitting in a New York subway car traveling between Coney Island and Times Square, Louis Stettner observed his fellow Americans. Equipped with a Rolleiflex that allowed him to lean over the viewfinder and avoid appearing aggressive, he took portraits of everyday commuters, alone or in groups of two: couples, friends, colleagues, family. Photography, on an amateur level, had been his passion for ten years already. Not the kind found in the illustrated press, then experiencing a boom, but that of the great masters, which he began to discover at the age of sixteen, flipping through back issues of *Camera Work* magazine, studying original prints by Paul Strand or Clarence H. White at the Metropolitan Museum of Art, or visiting Alfred Stieglitz's gallery, An American Place. "Through him, I came to realize that photography could be a major vehicle of expression, capable of communicating my most passionate feelings and experiences with the world around me. It was right up there with painting, sculpture and literature. He convinced me that photography could be worlds more than an indulgent hobby; one could, quite literally, dedicate one's life to

working in the medium."[2] Therefore, in 1939, Louis Stettner joined
the Photo League, an association of committed photographers
who promoted the work of Lewis Hine and embraced social and
artistic photography. Documentary photography in itself did not
interest him. It was people that fascinated him, and the telling
details that revealed them: facial expressions, gestures, poses, hands,
clothes. Unlike Walker Evans, whose subway series he was unaware
of, although it had been shot a few years earlier,[3] Louis Stettner
did not hide his camera and did not try to photograph passengers
unawares. Sid Grossman, photographer and founding member of the
Photo League, who published these images in the arts and literature
review *The New Iconograph*, noted: "The primary dramatic point [of his
photographs] is thus made the man rather than the incident. This
approach clearly makes his difference from photographers like Helen
Levitt, Morris Engel and Henri Bresson [sic], who work rather with
specific situations or relationships of the moment."[4]

This observation could be applied to many photographs by
Louis Stettner, who retained his empathetic approach throughout
his life. But his early subway series is also striking for its strict,
almost austere compositions, with a clearly defined frame, square in
this case, as symmetrical as possible. The mirroring or doubling that
is often found in Stettner's images has sometimes been linked to his
personal life, and in particular to his having an identical twin brother,
Irving.[5] The people in Louis Stettner's photographs often cross paths
or move toward or apart from each other, as if connected by a central
element in the image. A ghostly reflection appears in a store window,
two pairs of eyes overlap, a woman leans over a newspaper while her
neighbor ignores her book and looks directly at the camera.

When he took these portraits in 1946, Louis Stettner was twenty-
four years old. He had returned from the war, having photographed
the fighting in the Philippines and the ruins of Hiroshima. "If my
photographs have always been embedded in daily life, with the
emphasis on what is called 'the common man,' it is because my
early formative years were deeply politicized by world events. I
grew up with the rise of totalitarianism and was part of a hurried
transformation of the average citizen into a combat soldier. It was

the man in the street who confronted Hitler. From an artist mostly
concerned with aesthetics, I became a direct participant in the
passionate issues of our times. As a result, politics and art in my
photographs have always been intertwined."[6]

Most members of the Photo League had left-wing sensibilities,
and many of them were, like him, from immigrant Jewish families.
They also shared an elevated idea of photography as a means of
expression and were well versed in its history and its ongoing debates,
led by figures such as Elizabeth McCausland and Berenice Abbott.
Stettner, who had taken a course at the League with Max Drucker
in 1939, began teaching a course in basic techniques at the Photo
League in 1947. It was there that he learned, through his colleague
Walter Rosenblum, that the Parisian photographer Willy Ronis, also
Jewish and a Communist, wanted to stage an exhibition of French
photography in New York. No further encouragement was needed:
Louis Stettner decided to leave for Paris, where his brother Irving was
already living. In July 1947, he wrote to Willy Ronis, saying that he
would be in Paris at the end of the month and that he wanted to meet
up with him and gather the best of French photography, with a view
to an exhibition at the Photo League's gallery.

Paris: an artist's life · The imagined ideas of Paris that Louis Stettner
brought with him in July 1947 all dated from the pre-war period.
There were the photographs of Eugène Atget, which he knew through
the publications of Berenice Abbott. There were the steamy nights
of Henry Miller, who had been discovered by Stettner's book-loving
brother at the Gotham Book Mart, a store that sold copies of *Tropic
of Cancer* under the counter. And there was *Paris de nuit* by Brassaï, to
whom Stettner was introduced by Henry Miller shortly after arriving
in Paris. Echoing this ghostly past, Louis Stettner shot a photo essay
with an old view camera and large-format film, which he had sent
over from the U.S. Taking up lodgings on the rue des Feuillantines,
then the square de Châtillon, in the 14th *arrondissement*, he carried
his heavy camera around the neighborhood. His street photographs,
in which cars are almost entirely absent, seem unreal, as if the city
had been emptied of its inhabitants. This strangeness is reinforced

by a high-contrast print treatment, which recalls the filmmaking technique known as "day for night." "For Stettner is irremediably a city dweller. By this curious affinity which binds each temperament to a theme, to a predetermined subject, he finds his true element in the Capernaum of the big city, where all is art, artifice and intelligence, sweat and secretion of man … He does not allow himself to be seduced by the picturesque. … [He chooses] the dreary vulgar habitations, neither beautiful nor ugly, neither pleasant nor sinister, which he seizes from the most convenient angle and encloses in a network of vertical and horizontal lines with the rectitude and gravity of a geometrician."[7]

During the same period, Louis Stettner, guided by Willy Ronis, discovered the new French photography, which would later become known as humanist photography. After visiting the Salon National de la Photographie and meeting a number of his colleagues, he sent back to New York a selection of images by a dozen photographers in December 1947. Some of these went on to become iconic. Exhibited at the Photo League gallery in April 1948, they were accompanied by a text by the photography historian Beaumont Newhall, entitled "Chasseurs d'images." This was the first time Willy Ronis, Robert Doisneau and Édouard Boubat had been exhibited in the U.S., and the show was well received.[8] But while support for the Communist Party was at its height in France, the Cold War had begun in the U.S. The Photo League was therefore placed on the blacklist of subversive organizations, which led to its members facing discriminatory measures. Louis Stettner decided to remain in Paris.

He entered the world of art via his regular visits to the cafés of Montparnasse and Saint-Germain-des-Prés, and also thanks to the G.I. Bill, a program that helped U.S. soldiers demobilized after the Second World War by granting them a monthly allowance that could be used to pay for education. He briefly attended classes at the studio of the sculptor Ossip Zadkine, then enrolled at the Institut des Hautes Études Cinématographiques (IDHEC), because Paris did not yet have a school of photography. This gave him the opportunity to make two short films and to meet Léo Ferré, an unknown young musician, who composed a piece of music while watching Stettner's filmed footage of fairgrounds.[9] But photography remained Louis Stettner's true passion. He maintained longstanding friendships with Brassaï and Édouard Boubat, regularly saw Paul Strand, Robert Frank and William Eugene Smith, and got to know the Swedish photographers Rune Hassner and Tore Johnson. "I would take long daily walks with my camera, leaving myself open to whatever happened around me. […] There was no economic basis and the possibility of recognition was slight. I suppose I was driven by a great need and love to get close to the world around me. Each photograph was a way of reaching out, an act of discovery."[10] Pursuing his own ideas, he took a large number of photographs and dreamed of turning them into two books. Captivated by passersby viewed from behind, whose fleeting and mysterious nature he tried to capture, he sometimes flirted with surrealism. His image of a girl dressed for her first communion, which rather recalls Jean Vigo's film *L'Atalante*, was praised and published in the magazine *Modern Photography*.[11] The one he entitled "Family Walking (Ménage)" was exhibited at the 1950 Salon National de la Photographie in Paris and seven of his pictures were included in the exhibition *Subjektive Fotografie* in Sarrebruck, Germany, the following year. Some of his images from this period recall the work of Robert Doisneau in their subject matter, including the two boys in the street in Aubervilliers, but most are differentiated from French-style humanism by their lack of anecdote or witty or sentimental connotations.

However, his allowance was not enough to live on, Paris was still suffering postwar hardships, and despite the acclaim he received for a fine portfolio with an introduction by Brassaï, Stettner only managed to survive thanks to the help of his elder brother, David. The situation seemed to improve in 1950 when the Economic Cooperation Administration, which oversaw the Marshall Plan, offered him work in Paris and in Norway, but Stettner lost the job when the U.S. Embassy discovered his links with the Photo League. After unsuccessful attempts to find a publisher for his proposed books on Paris, and despite having recently won an award for young photographers from *Life* magazine, alongside Elliott Erwitt, Dennis Stock, Robert Frank, and Ruth Orkin, he decided to return to New

York. On October 9, 1952, he boarded the ship M.V. *Italia* in Le Havre and arrived in New York nine days later. "Paris, probably the most beautiful city in the world, has been to me a living memorial to the dignity of human beings and what they are capable of,"[12] wrote Louis Stettner, who remembered this period in Paris as one of the happiest of his life. It was there that he chose to return with his family forty years later, to experience a new phase in his artistic life.

New York: city of contrasts · "New York! How can I describe a city that has nourished me. A city I love, a city that forgives nothing but accepts everyone."[13] Stettner soon rediscovered the grandeur of the New York skies. The city inspired the photograph that is not his most representative but remains his best-known: the shot of a man lying back in the sunshine on Brooklyn Promenade, with his head thrown back and arms outstretched, against a backdrop of the Manhattan skyline. Louis Stettner's work is full of people sitting on benches, lying on the ground, or soaking up the sun. "People are more interesting to me when their bodies are calm and relaxed, rather than when they're rushing around,"[14] he said. Instead of Henri Cartier-Bresson's "decisive moment," his pictures often capture moments of immobility or inaction, when not much or nothing at all is happening. "His work stands in direct opposition to photojournalism: the latter is more like a pictorial representation of an incident that, however interesting it may be, is always fleeting, forgotten as soon as the image is out of sight. Stettner is interested in the enduring and universal nature of his subjects,"[15] observed the journalist James McGovern. This apparently singular style earned him a solo exhibition in 1954 at the legendary Limelight Gallery, the first gallery in postwar New York to be dedicated solely to the masters of photography.

In Stettner's images of both New York and Paris, we often find the composition crisscrossed with lines that may either separate or connect people to their surroundings in an unusual way. Gazes are often hidden or invisible: figures are viewed from behind, their faces concealed by a pillar, a hat, a shadow. This gives some of his shots a freeze-frame quality. These graphic effects are exaggerated still further in his series *Penn Station*. Diagonal lines, signage, lettering,

numbers, light effects, and scenes glimpsed behind glass, as if in
a dream, combined to create an ode to travel, intersections, and
interconnection, yet reflecting an ongoing lack of communication
between people.

Louis Stettner lived in Manhattan at this time and Weegee,
with whom he made a rare audio recording,[16] was one of his closest
friends. In 1956, he did a residency at Yaddo, an artists' community
in Saratoga Springs, New York, where he met the writer Saul Bellow.
As a reader of Walt Whitman, Herman Melville, Jean Genet, Arthur
Rimbaud and Henry Miller, he could not help being interested by the
emergence of the Beat Generation, who questioned the foundations
of the American dream. In 1958, he recorded the everyday life
of Nancy Miller, a nineteen-year-old beatnik. Nancy rejected the
bourgeois way of life and lived from day to day among artists and
bohemians, wandering the streets and cafés of Greenwich Village
and hanging around with jazz musicians. Some images from this
series were published in the magazine *Pageant* in March 1959, under
the title "The Cool Life." Stettner himself began to combine writing,
traveling, and sculpture, and in the 1960s became increasingly
politicized, taking part in protests for human rights and against
the war in Vietnam. A member of the Communist Party, he was
under FBI surveillance from 1969 to 1977. "New York City is where
I have lived for most of my life, amidst the smoke, fumes, the
bustle, and the still moments or stray corners that have sometimes
touched eternity. […] I am profoundly moved by its lyric beauty and
horrified by its cruelty and suffering."[17] His images of protests and
demonstrations reflect his deep inner revulsion at the injustices
suffered by workers, women, and Black communities. As an artist,
he was extremely outspoken about the establishment and about
comtemporary trends in photography. He also took an active role in
critical, artistic, and cultural debates, most notably via his column
Speaking Out, later renamed *A Humanist View*, which was published
in the magazine *Camera 35*. In these articles, he loudly and clearly
promoted the humanist realism movement, which had fallen out of
vogue with photography's institutions. His series *Workers*, a collection
of portraits of people working in factories, nonetheless became a

critical success and was featured in several exhibitions. At the same time, he continued to explore the city, recording it in an ever more fragmented fashion, with the driving aim of "producing a photograph that will be an experience rather than a document. […] By using only a head or arm juxtaposed against an object in the environment, such as tree, plant, doorway, etc., we can come up with a sum total photograph—that is not a record of reality, but an interpretation of what was seen,"[18] he explained. His shots of New York in the 1980s and 1990s also record the poverty and loneliness that could be seen on the streets, particularly in his series *On the Bowery*.

The wider world calls · Although he remained deeply attached to his two favorite cities, throughout his life Louis Stettner continued to feel the urge to travel and experience new things, both personally and artistically. Between 1947 and 1952, he visited Austria, Italy, Spain, and the south of France. His friendship with Swedish photographers led to a solo exhibition in Stockholm in 1959, and up to 1965, he spent long periods in Portugal, the UK, Spain, France, Greece, and the Netherlands, where he worked for the press and in advertising, as well as writing novels, short stories, and plays. His photographic work, in this period, was more focused on bodies and gestures. Two fishermen in Ibiza inspired the photo essay *Pepe and Tony, Spanish Fishermen* (ca. 1960–1962). Stettner also visited Mexico, the Soviet Union, East Germany, Cuba, and later, Chile.

Then in 1990 came the big move. Louis Stettner and his wife Janet, with their two children, left New York and moved to Saint-Ouen, France, where they bought a house from friends and collectors Michel and Michèle Auer. "It felt like coming home. The children went to the local school and in a few months were speaking fluent French. […] Living here has proved to be one of the most creative periods in my life,"[19] he said. For more than twenty-five years, Louis Stettner devoted himself to collage, sculpture, painting, and drawing, while continuing to take photographs in black and white and sometimes in color. He still wandered through New York on summer vacations to Manhattan and to Athens, a small town on the Hudson River where the Stettners had a house. Due to rising demand for his

prints from collectors and museums, he revisited and organized his
archives. A darkroom at the end of his garden allowed him to make
his own prints, painstakingly creating a new interpretation of his
images. He varied the format of his cameras, sometimes returning
to a square format or a view camera.

"I think my first significant picture was one that I took when I was
fourteen years old. It was in the yard outside my home in Brooklyn.
It was winter, there was only a bare tree, snow, and a kind of wooden
fence. That was enough."[20] Louis Stettner's fascination with trees,
especially their trunks, is obvious, and this motif reappeared regularly
throughout his long life. He often treated it in an unusual way,
cropping off the tops of trees or positioning them in the center of the
image. Back in the 1970s, the landscapes of Montana and Wyoming
had inspired him to shoot a series on nature, and right at the end
of his life, it was the trees of Les Alpilles in France that revived his
urge to take pictures. He spent three years doing that, until a few
months before his death, using a bulky view camera to capture every
nuance of light. "I'm always happy in the forest, that's my idea of
joy. I visited Les Alpilles thirteen times! I think the place cast a spell
on me," he marveled. "There's nowhere else where nature expresses
its imagination so well. Battered by the mistral winds, the thick
trunks of the trees show their force of will. I've never managed to
photograph the forest anywhere else. It's a magical place."[21]

This final homage to the power of nature seems like the
culmination of a journey driven by freedom, resistance to oppression,
empathy, and the joy of being alive. Louis Stettner died in 2016,
a month after receiving the honor of a major retrospective at the
Centre Pompidou. He left behind him a body of work that has not
yet revealed all of its mysteries and treasures.

Notes

1   Louis Stettner, "The Creative Approach," *Camera 35*, July 1976.

2   Louis Stettner, "An American Contradiction," *Camera 35*, November 1974.

3   Walker Evans' subway series would not be widely seen until the publication of his book *Many Are Called* in 1966.

4   Sid Grossman, "Louis Stettner," *The New Iconograph*, Autumn 1947.

5   Clément Chéroux, "Beyond the Double Bind," in *Louis Stettner: Traveling Light*, Paris: Cernunnos/Dargaud, 2018.

6   Louis Stettner, *Wisdom Cries Out in the Streets*, Paris: Flammarion, 1999.

7   Brassaï, introduction to the portfolio *10 Photographs by Louis Stettner*, Paris & New York: Two Cities Publications, 1949.

8   "France: Through French Cameras," *The New York Times*, April 11, 1948; *Photo Notes*, Photo League, June 1948.

9   *Louis Stettner: Sophisme, Photographies 1990–1999*, Neuchâtel: Ides et Calendes, 1999. The piece of music was turned into the song "Les Forains," first recorded by Léo Ferré in 1950 for the Communist label Le Chant du Monde.

10   Louis Stettner, *Wisdom Cries Out in the Streets*.

11   Harry Roskolenko, "Louis Stettner," *Modern Photography*, August 1950.

12   Louis Stettner, letter to David Stettner, undated, Louis Stettner Archives.

13   Louis Stettner, *Wisdom Cries Out in the Streets*.

14   Louis Stettner, in *Ici ailleurs*, Paris: Éditions du Centre Pompidou/Éditions Xavier Barral, 2016.

15   James McGovern, "Un artiste américain. Louis Stettner et sa conception de l'art," *Photo Cinéma*, no. 566, December 1948.

16   Louis Stettner (prod.), *Famous Photographers Tell How*, New York: Candid Recordings, 1958.

17   Louis Stettner, *Wisdom Cries Out in the Streets*.

18   Louis Stettner, "People in parts," undated, unpublished, Louis Stettner archives.

19   Louis Stettner, *Wisdom Cries Out in the Streets*.

20   Louis Stettner, interview with Michèle Auer, in *Sophisme*.

21   Louis Stettner, in *Ici ailleurs*.

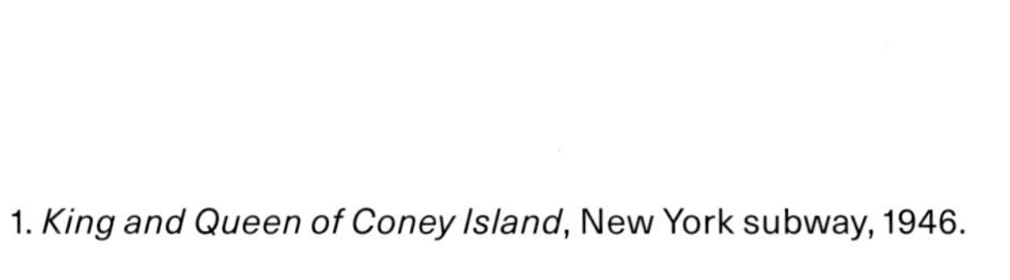

1. *King and Queen of Coney Island*, New York subway, 1946.

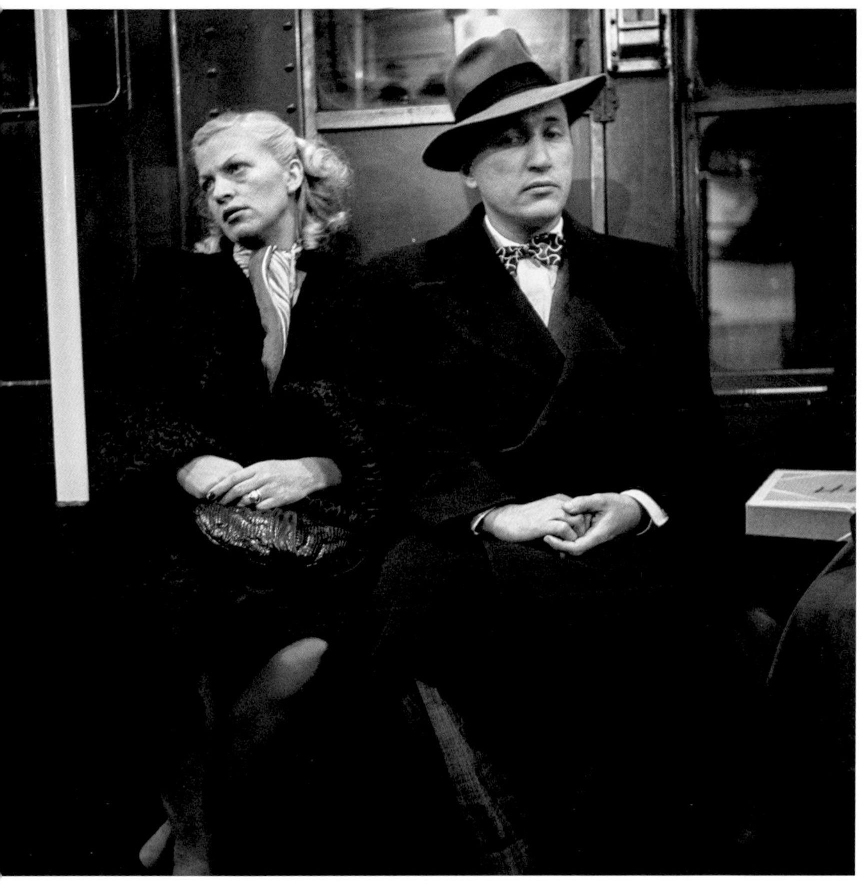

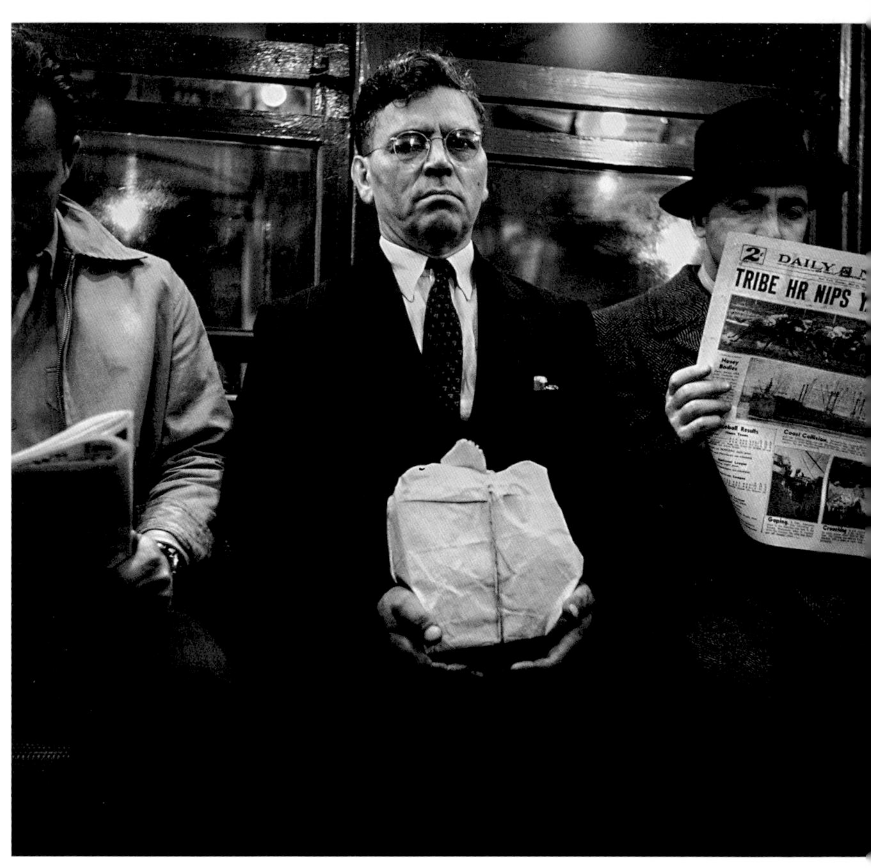

2. New York subway, 1946.

3. New York subway, 1946.

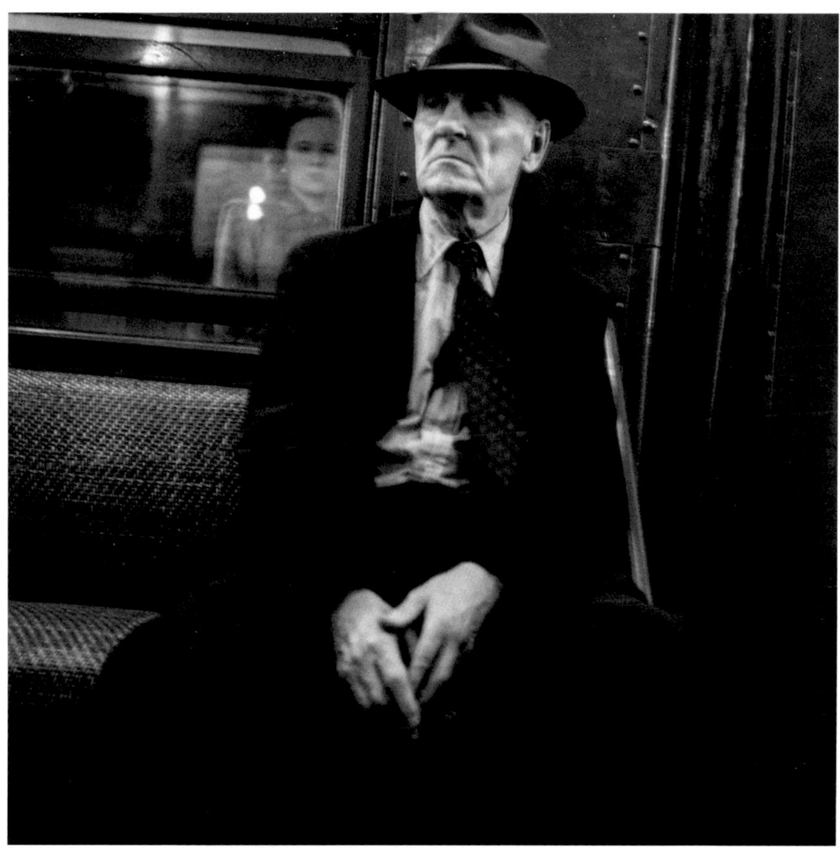

4. New York subway, 1946.

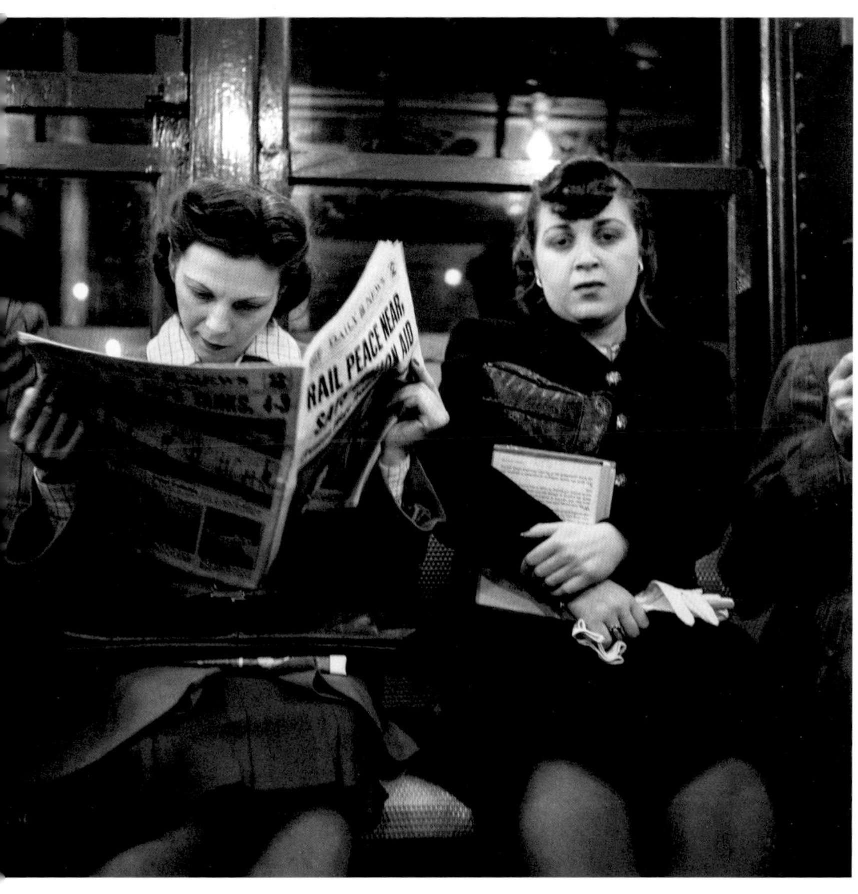
DAILY NEWS
NAIL PEACE NEAR,
ON AID

5. New York subway, 1946.

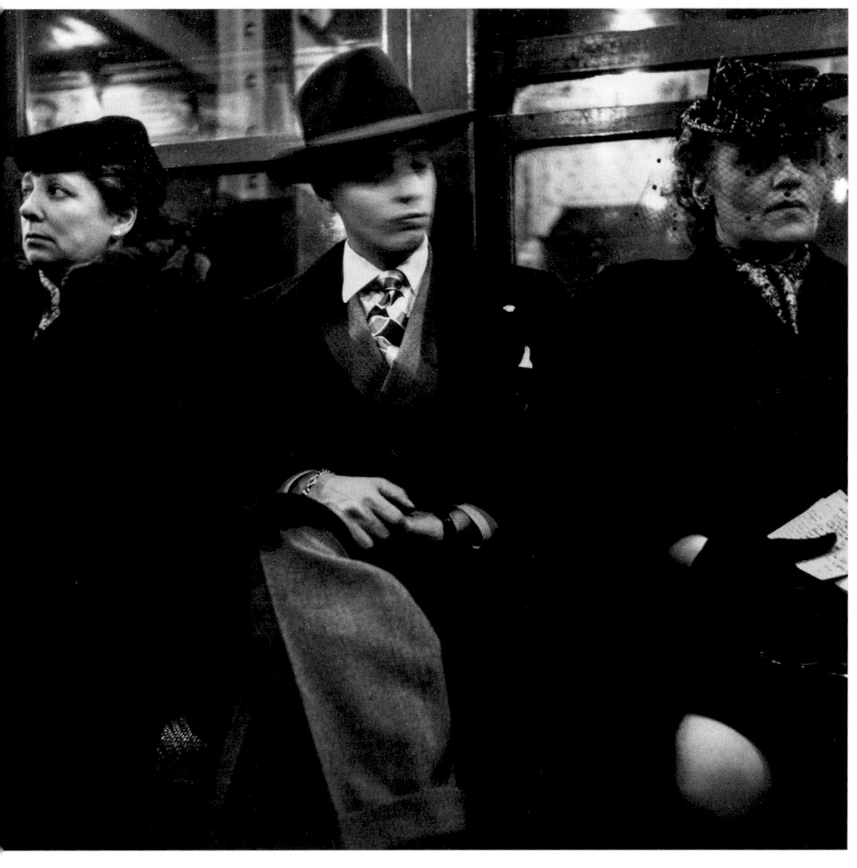

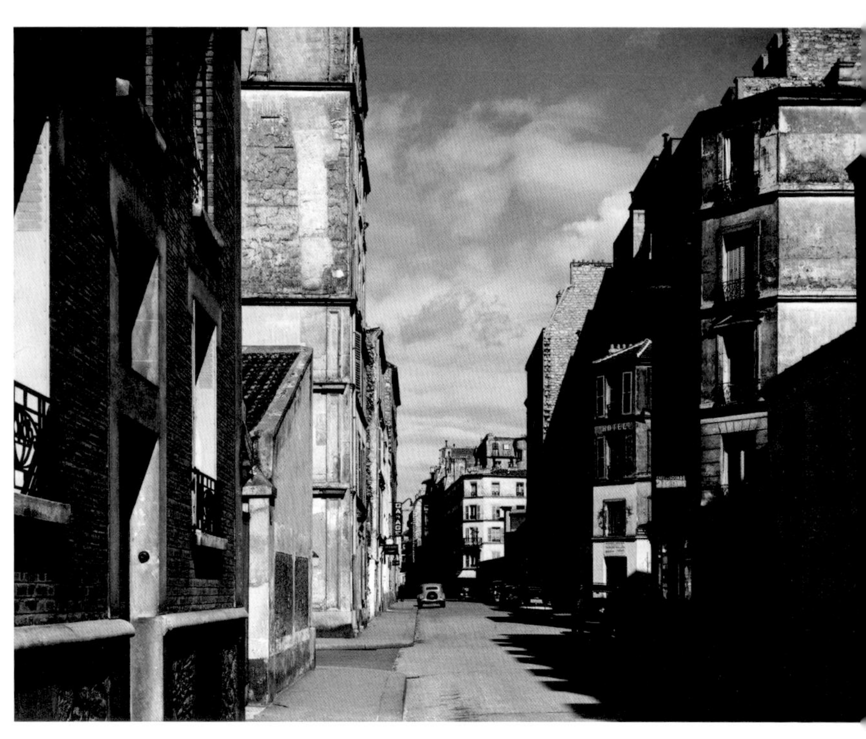

6. Rue Hippolyte-Maindron, Paris, ca. 1947–1949.

7. France, ca. 1947–1949.

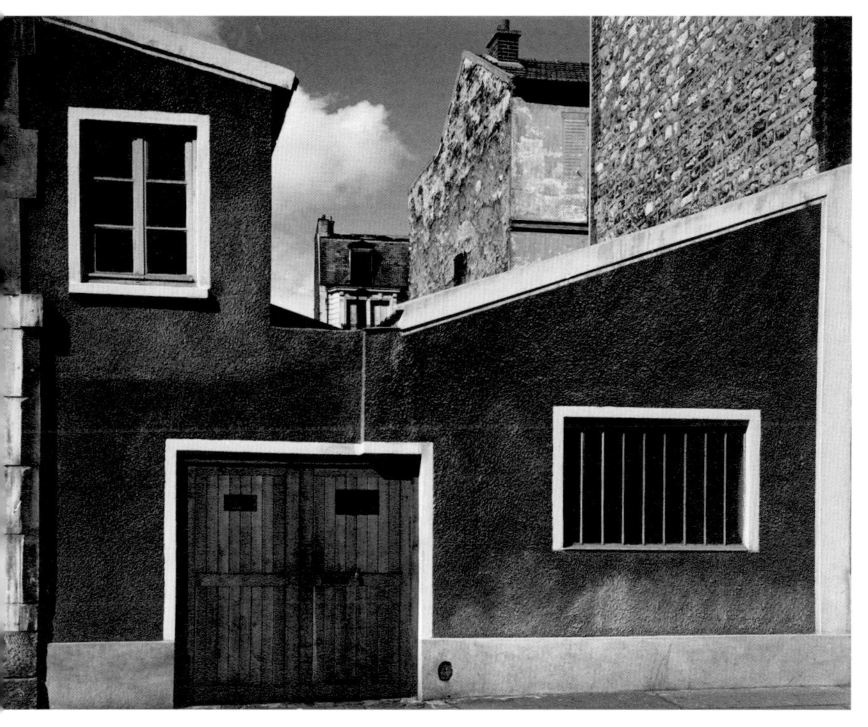

8. Châtillon's Home, 11, Square de Châtillon, Paris, ca. 1948–1949.

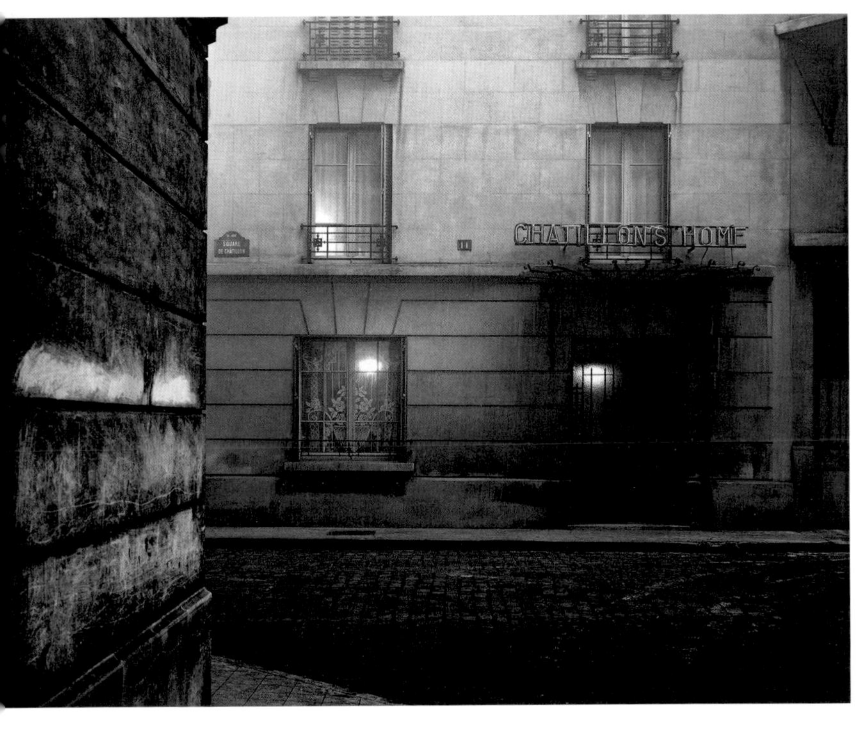

SQUARE
DE CHATILLON
11
CHATILLON'S HOME

9. Window display, Paris, ca. 1947–1952.

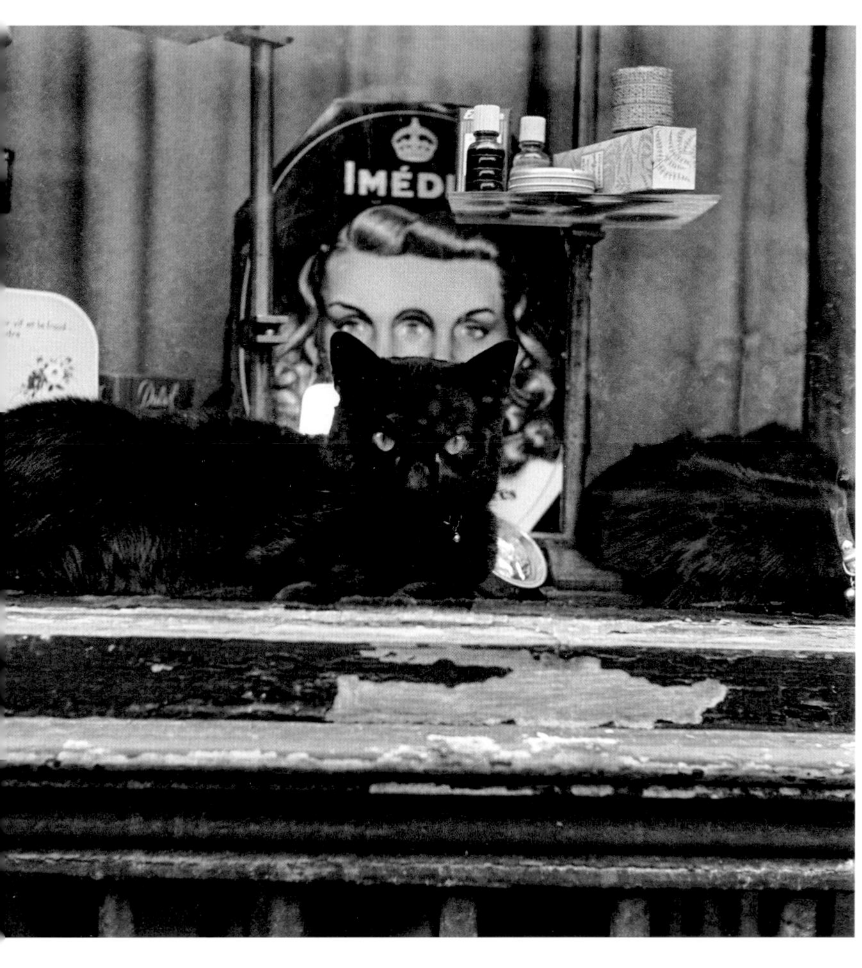
IMÉDI

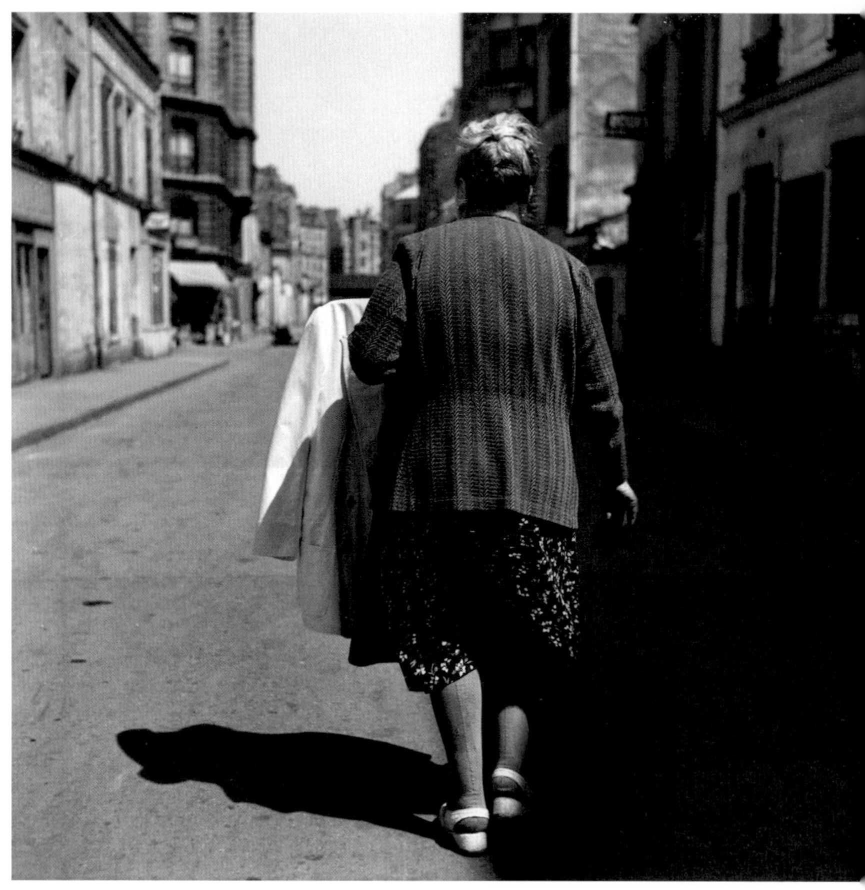

10. Passerby, Paris, ca. 1947–1952.

11. Communion, Paris, ca. 1947–1950.

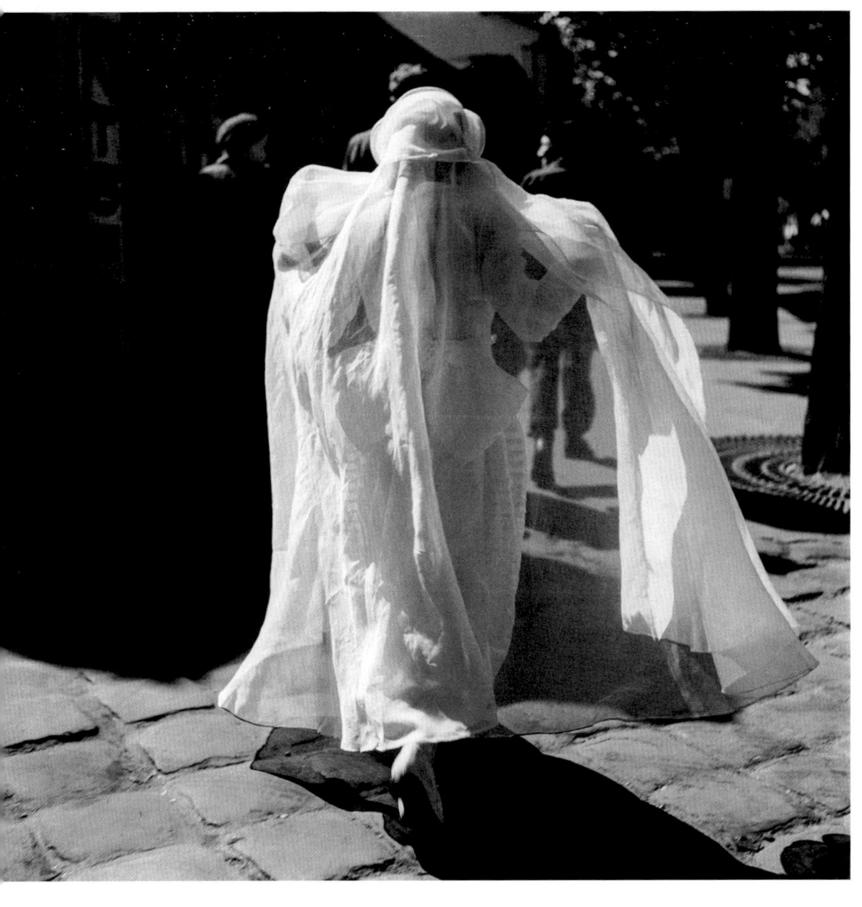

12. Family walking (*Ménage*), Paris, ca. 1947–1950.

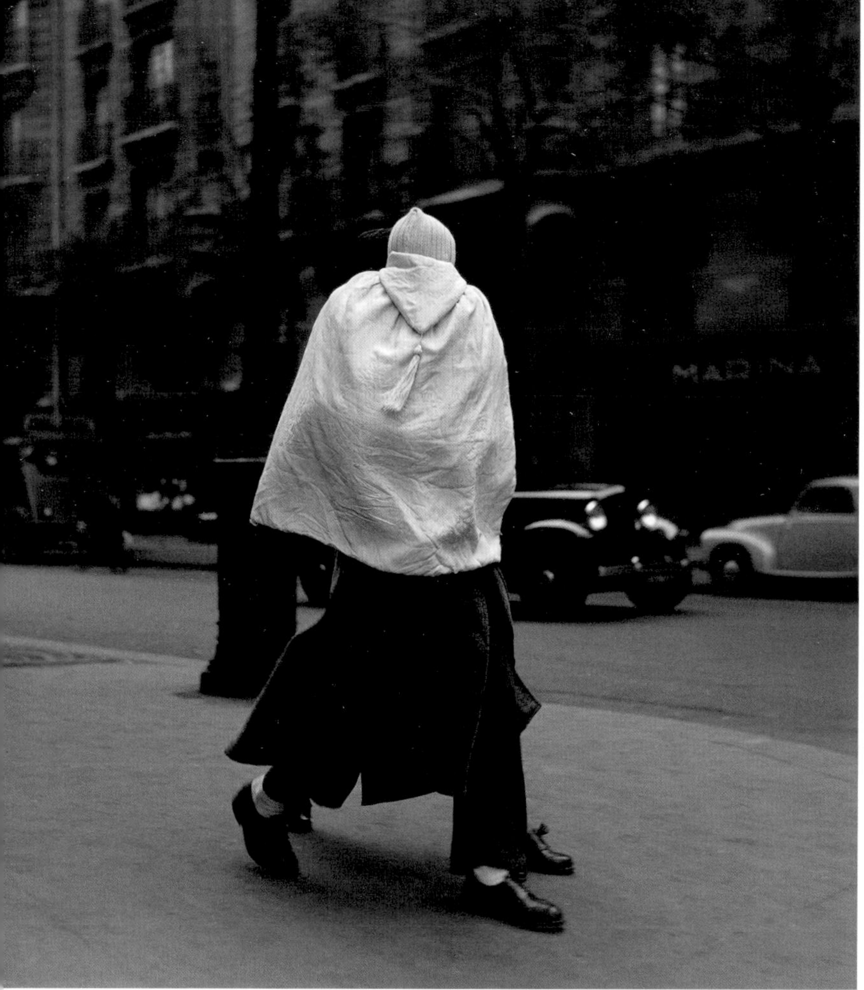
MARINA

13. British tourists, Place du Louvre, Paris, ca. 1947–1951.

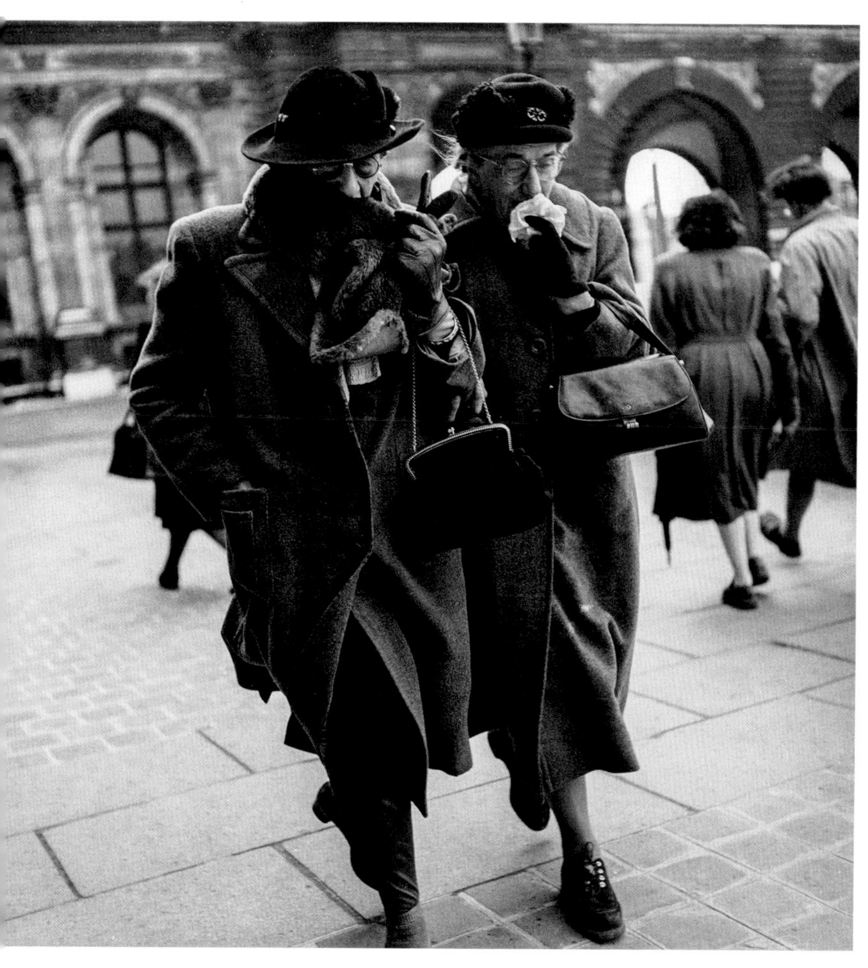

14. Near Pont Neuf, Paris, ca. 1947–1952.

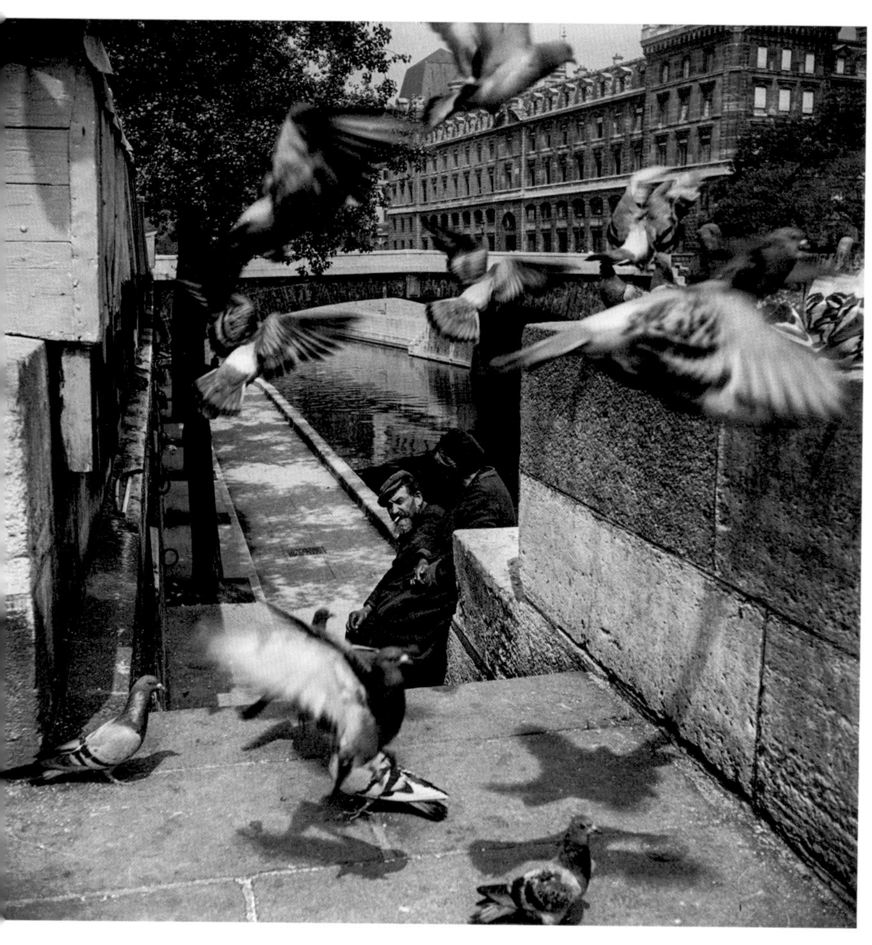

15. Aubervilliers, ca. 1947–1949.

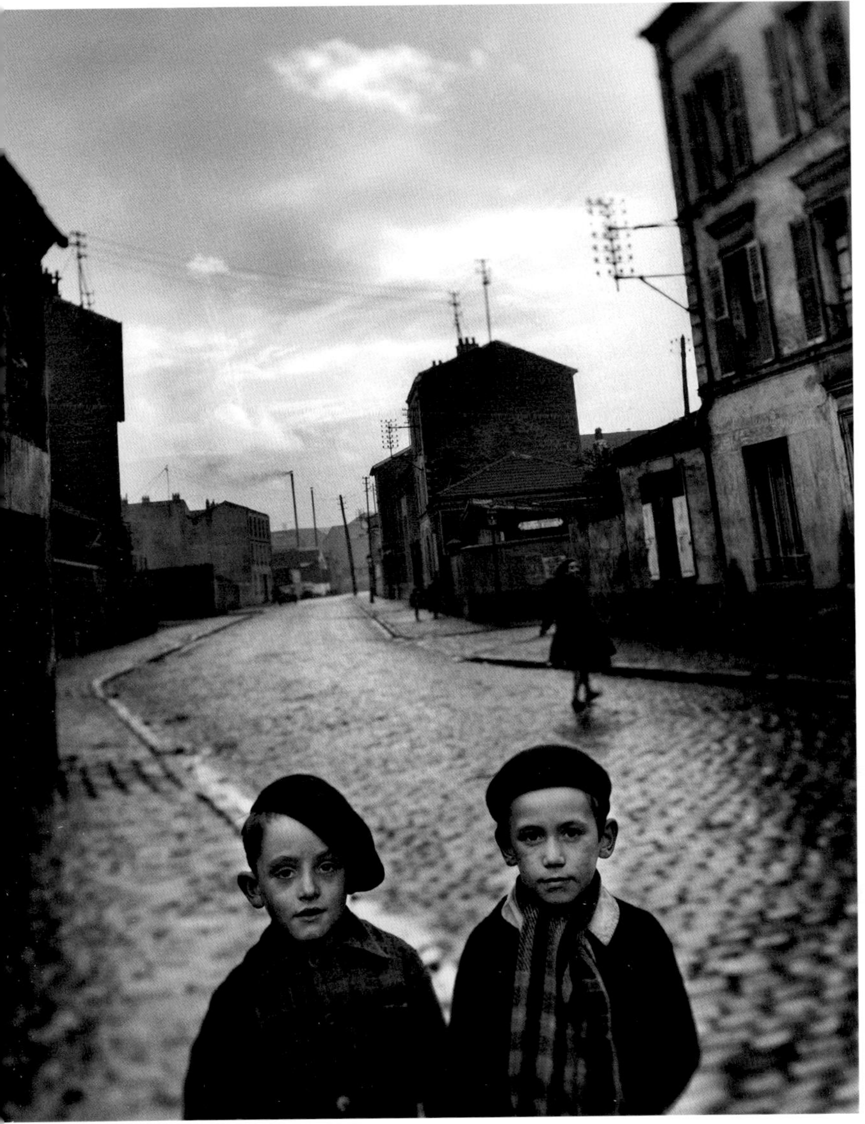

16. Avenue de Châtillon, Paris, ca. 1947–1949.

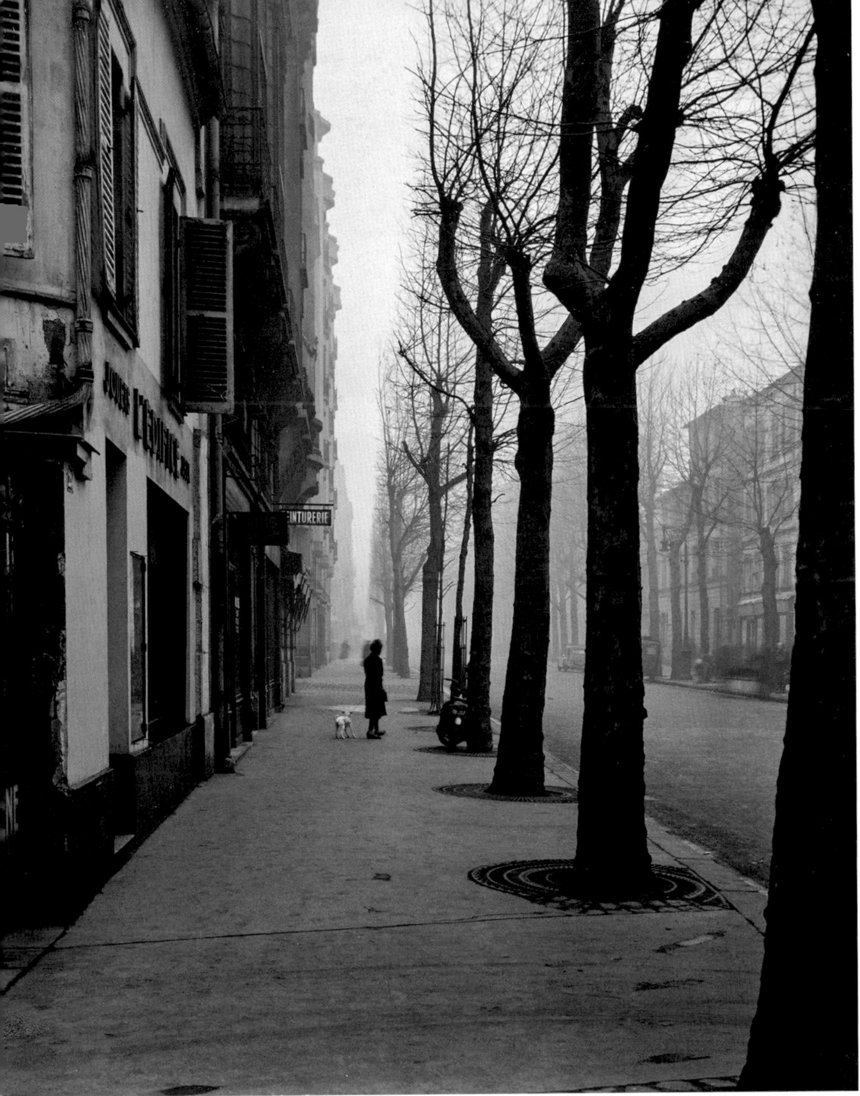
L'ENFANT
EINTURERIE

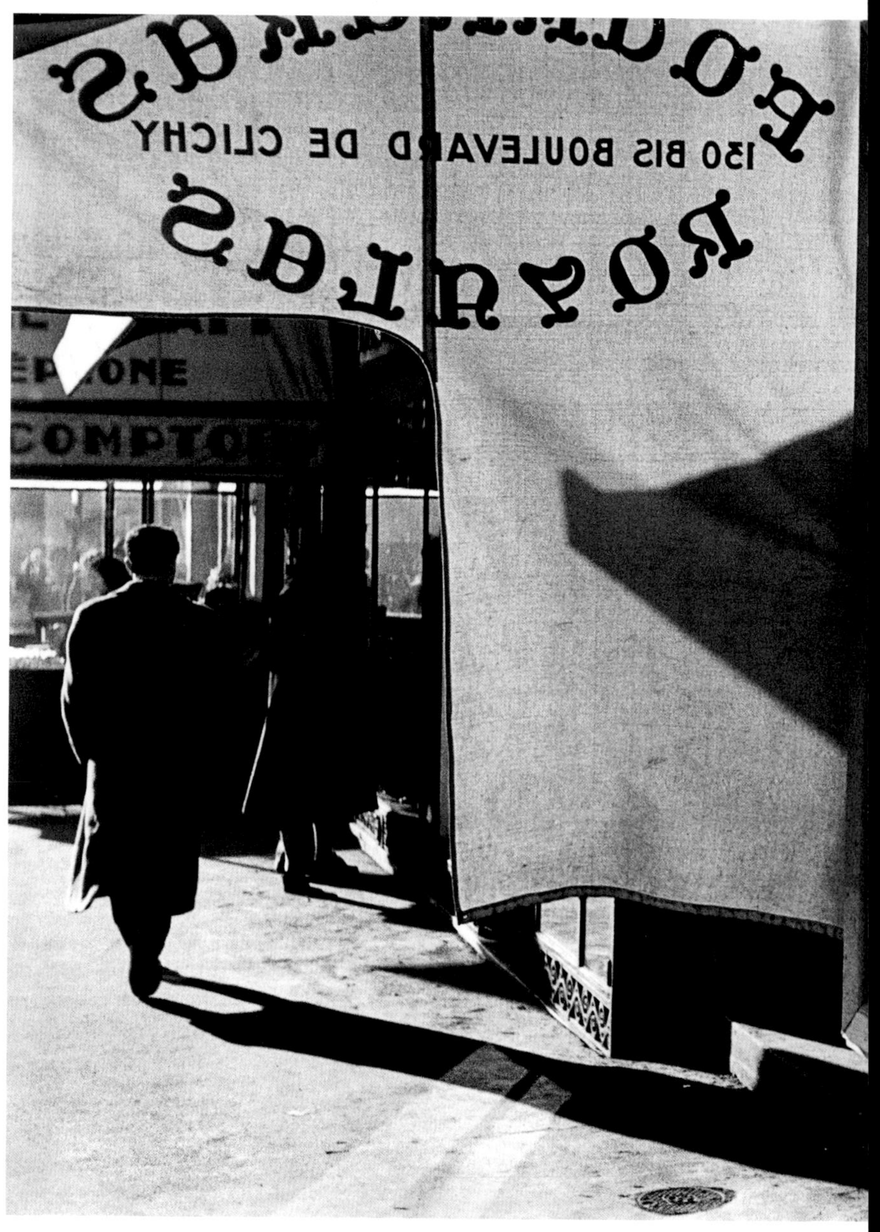

17. Boulevard de Clichy, Paris, ca. 1950–1952.

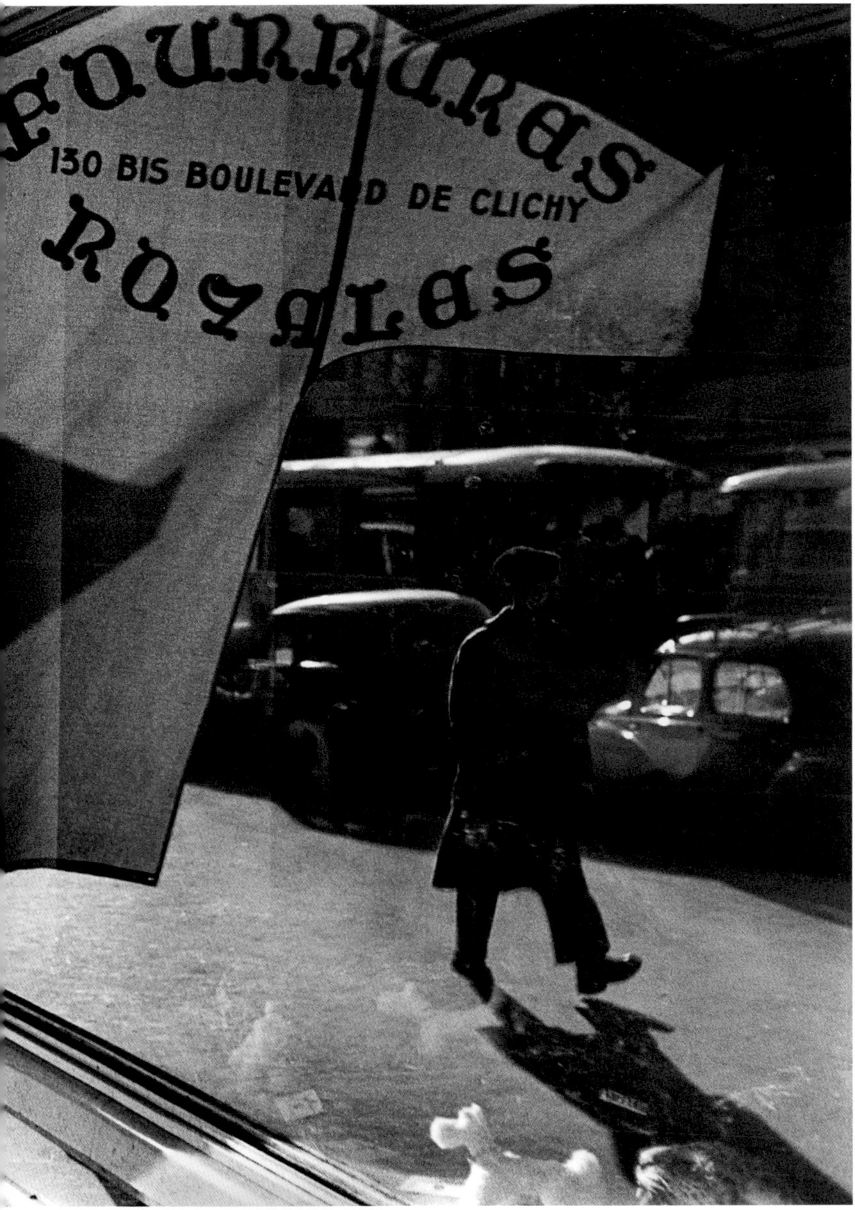

FOURRURES

130 BIS BOULEVARD DE CLICHY

ROZALES

18. Third Avenue El, New York, ca. 1952.

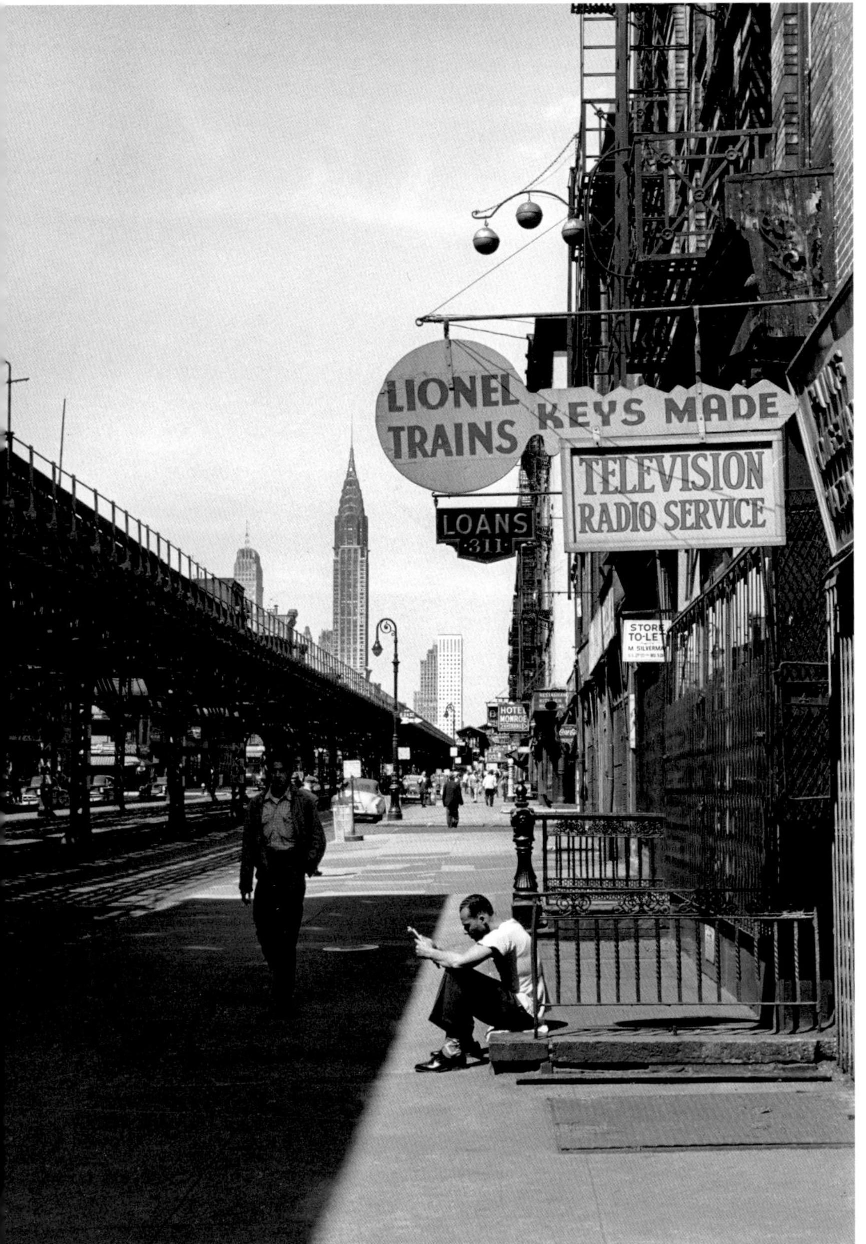

LIONEL TRAINS
KEYS MADE
TELEVISION RADIO SERVICE
LOANS ·311·
STORE TO-LET
M. SILVERMA
HOTEL MONROE
Coca-Cola

19. Brooklyn Promenade, New York, 1954.

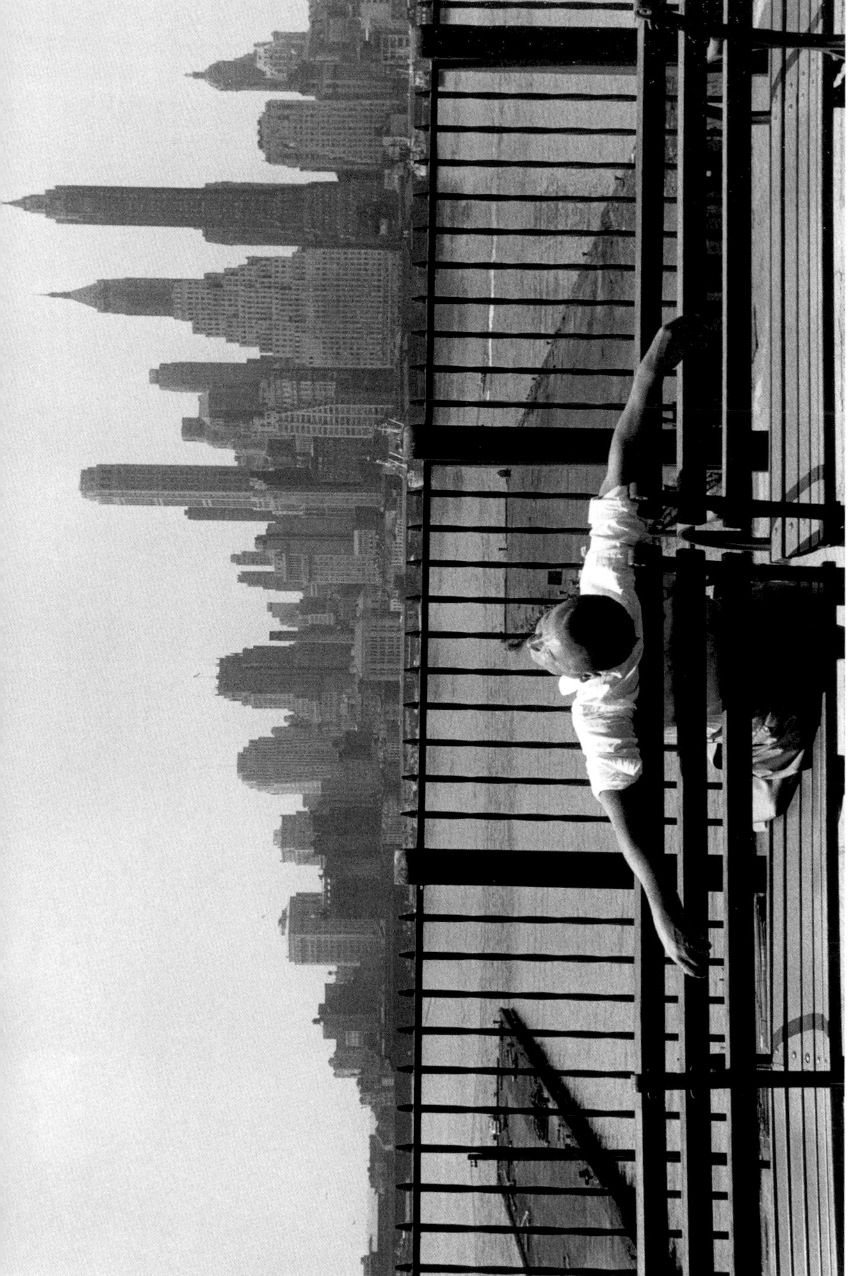

20. Under the El, Lower Second Avenue, New York, ca. 1954.

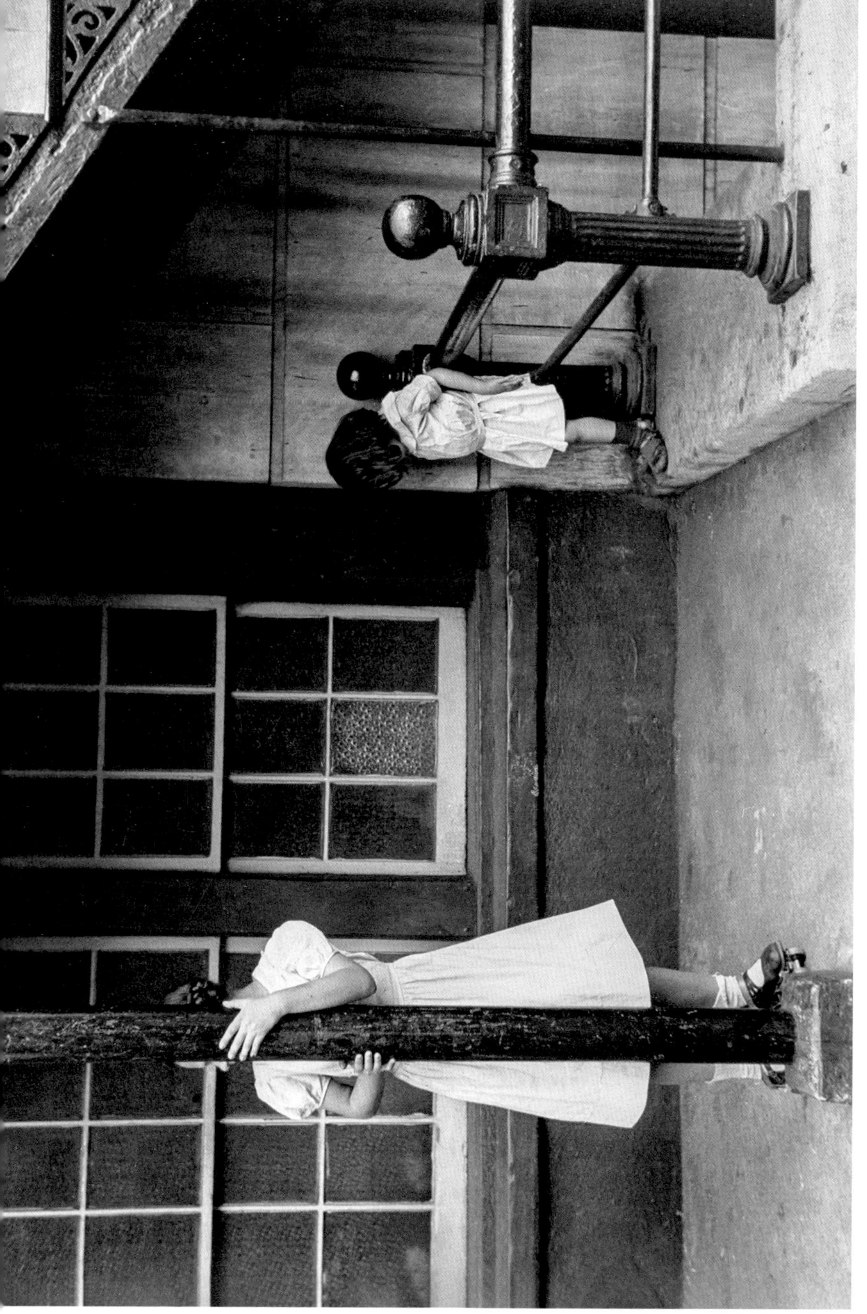

21. *Fifties Graffiti*, New York, ca. 1954–1956.

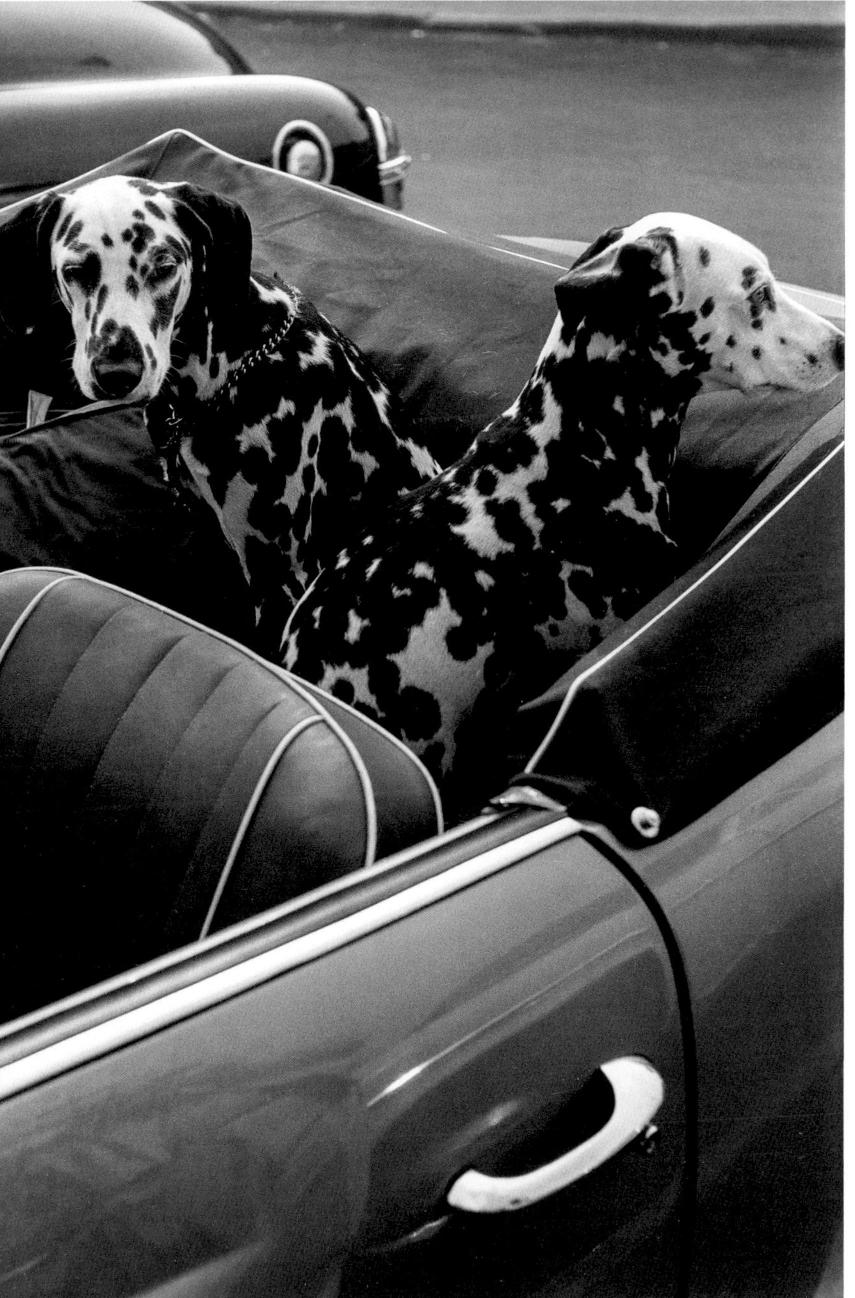

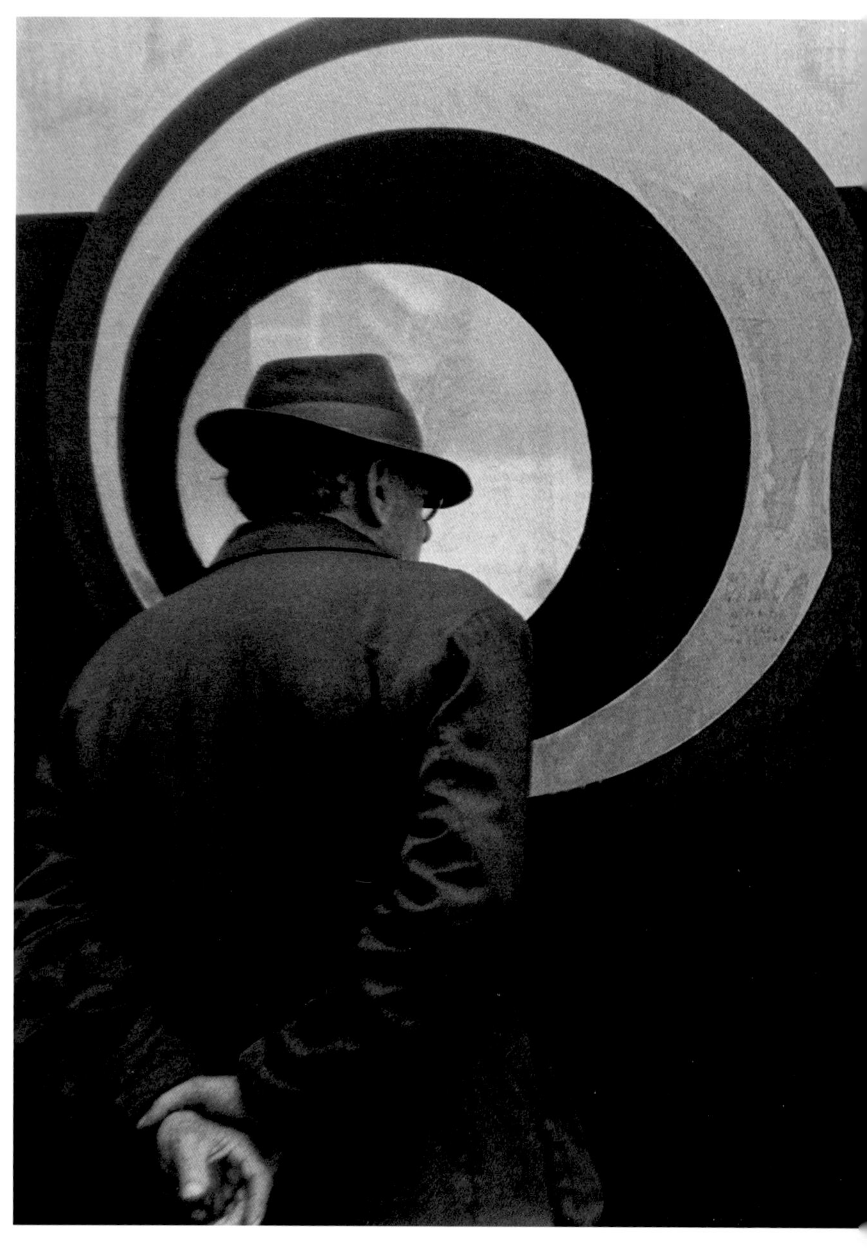

22. *Concentric Circles (Construction Site)*, New York, ca. 1952.

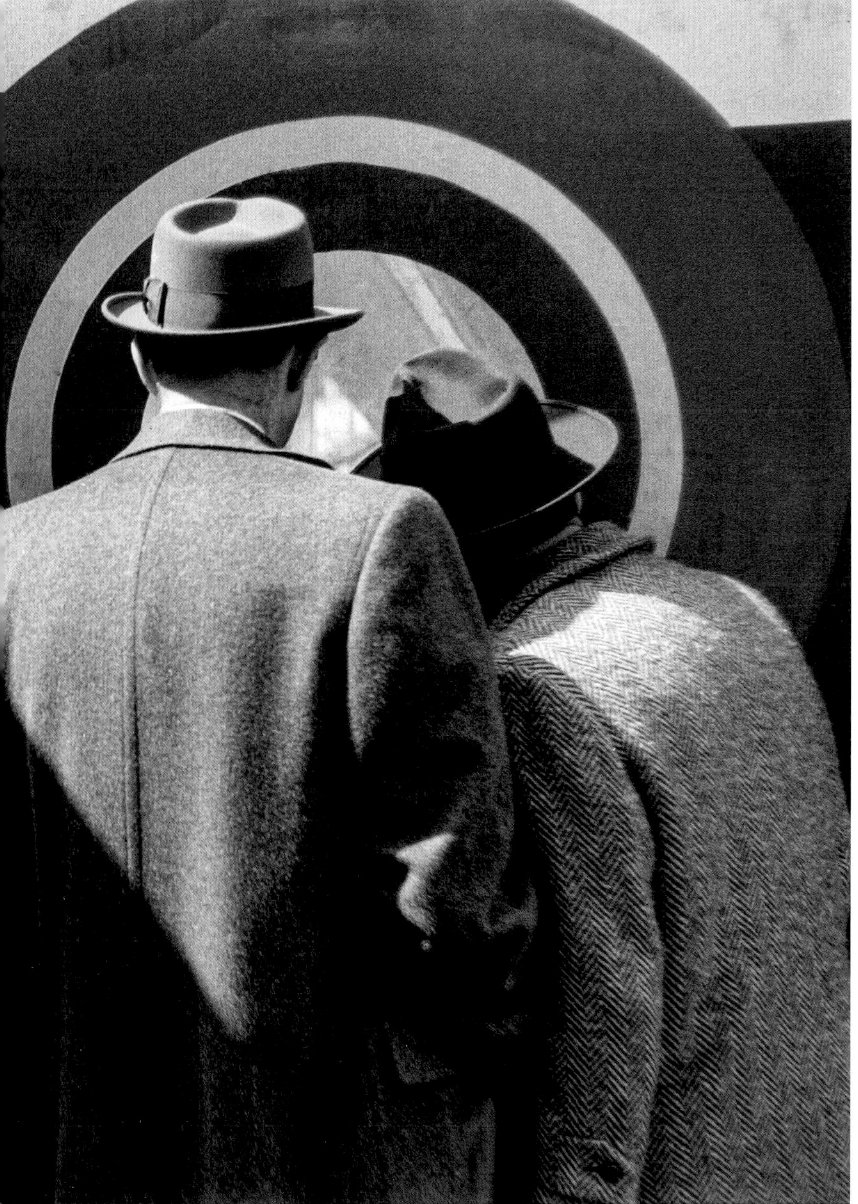

23. 84 Broadway, New York, ca. 1954.

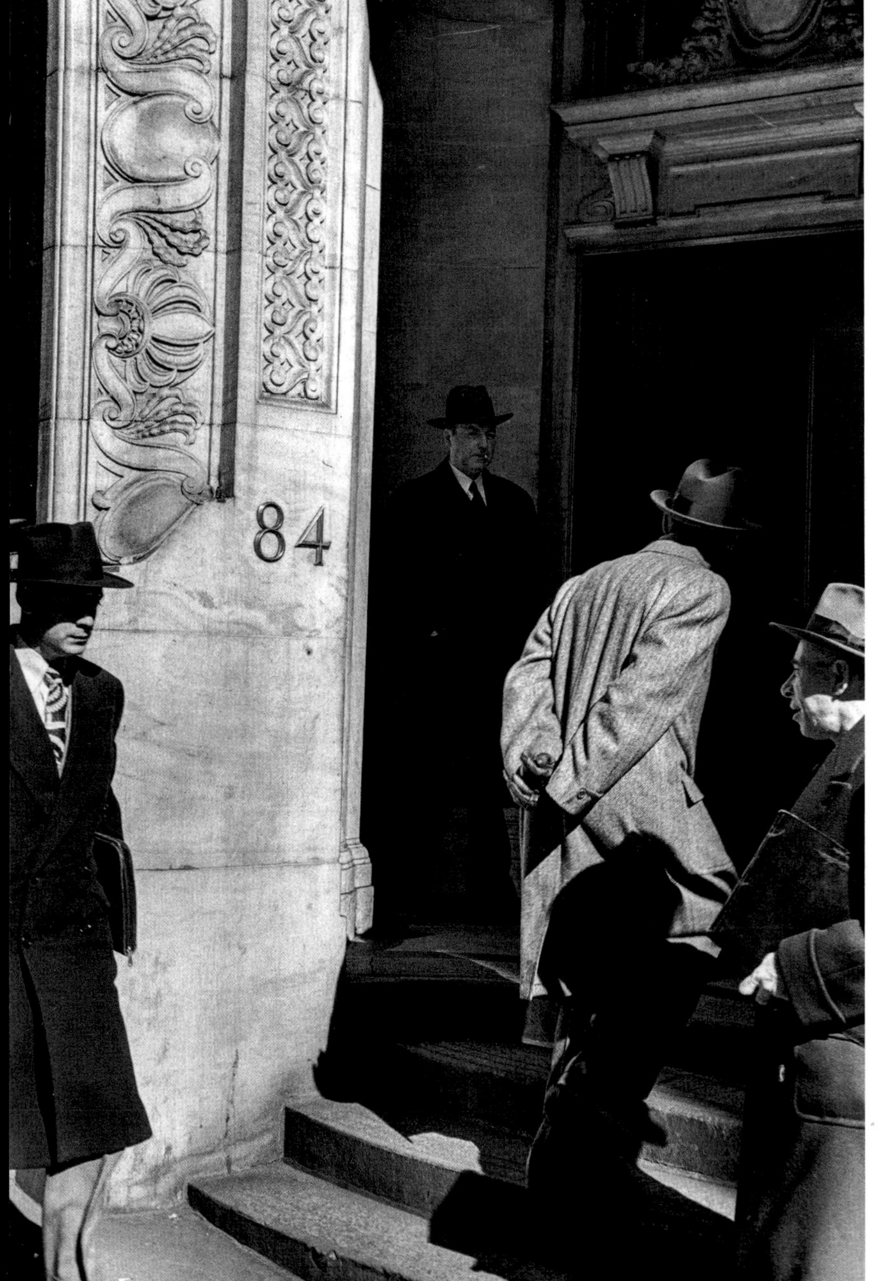

24. *Girl Playing in Circles*, Penn Station, New York, ca. 1952–1954.

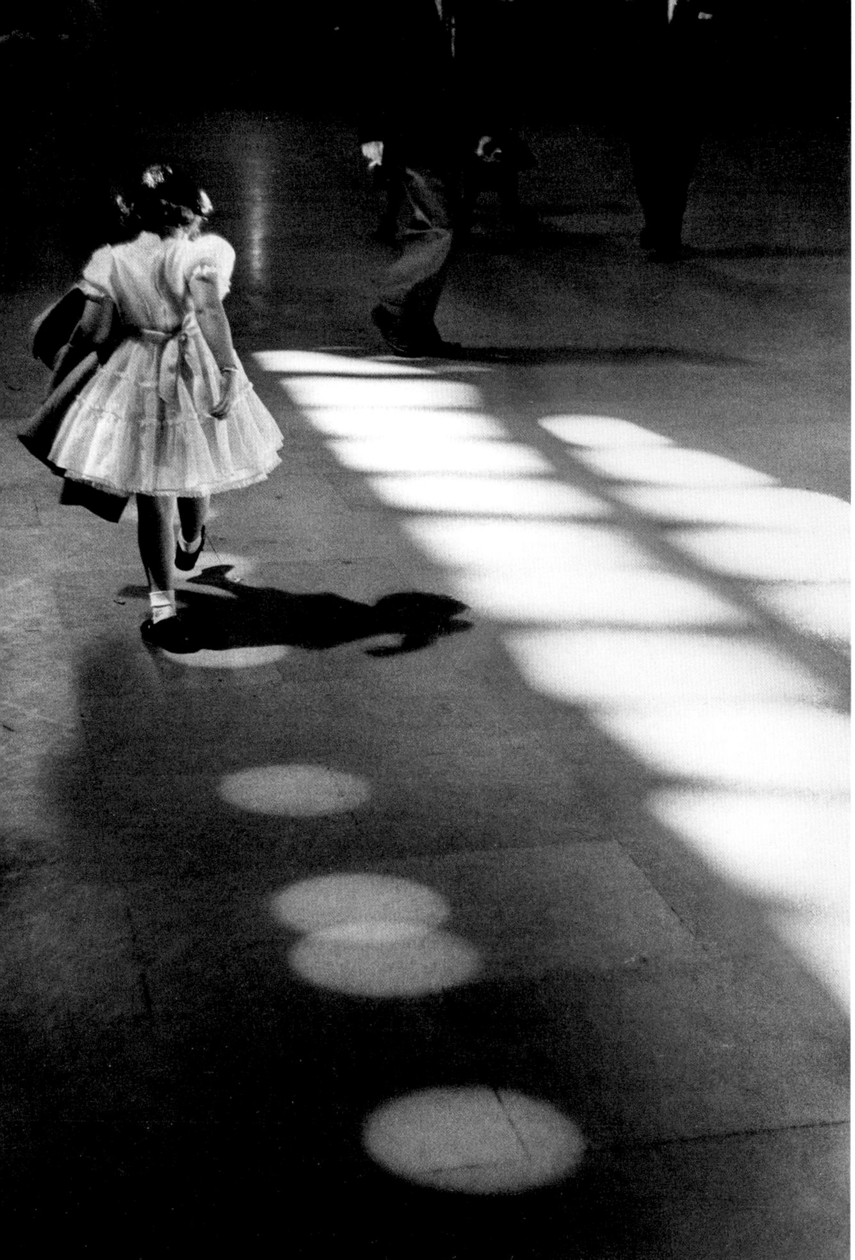

25. Penn Station, New York, 1958.

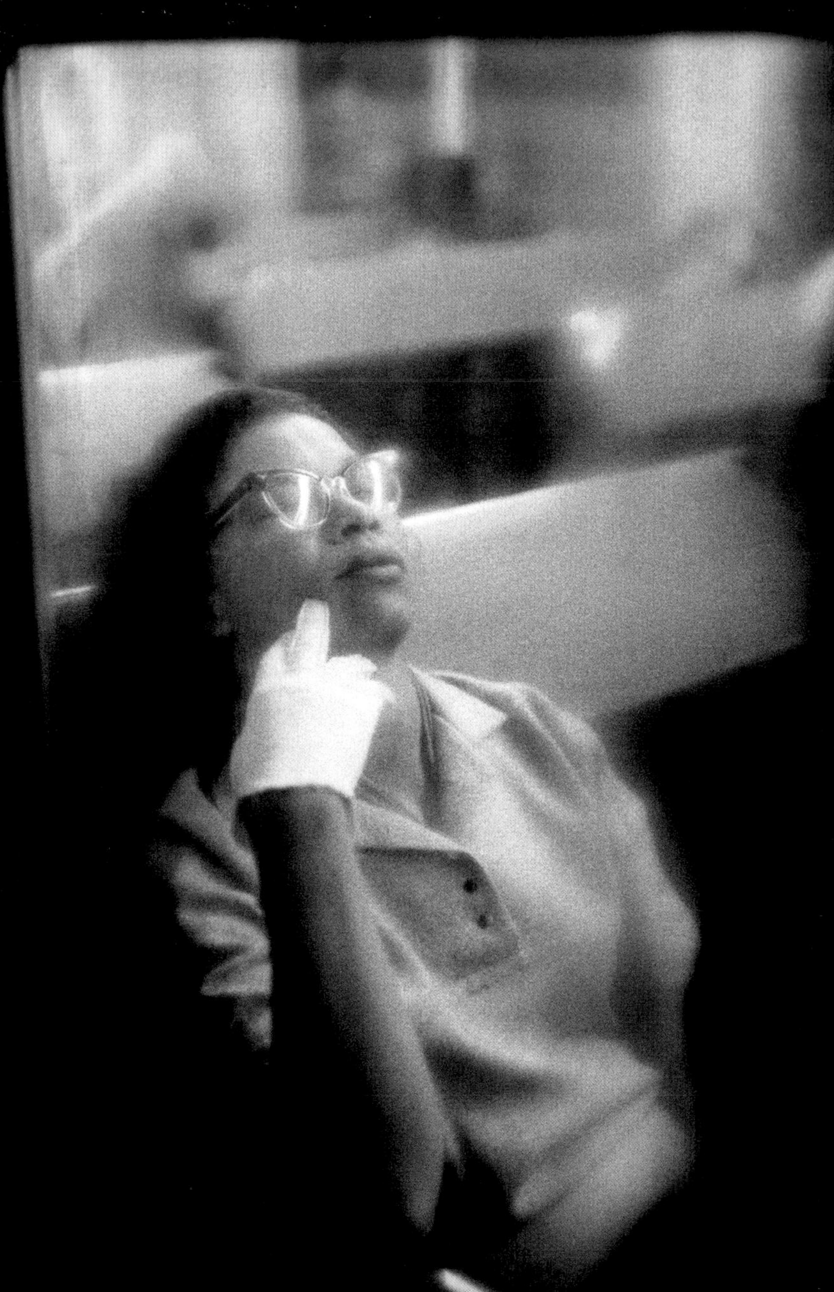

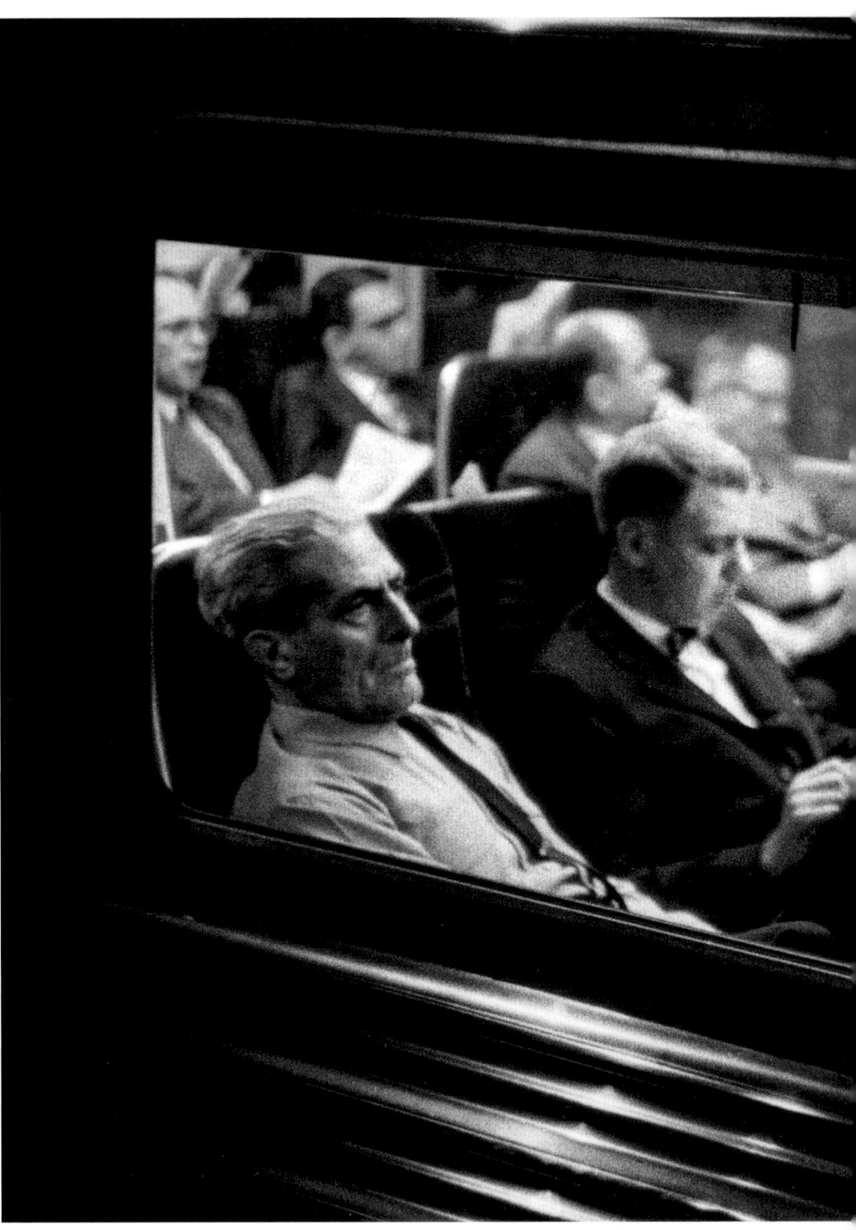

26. Penn Station, New York, 1958.

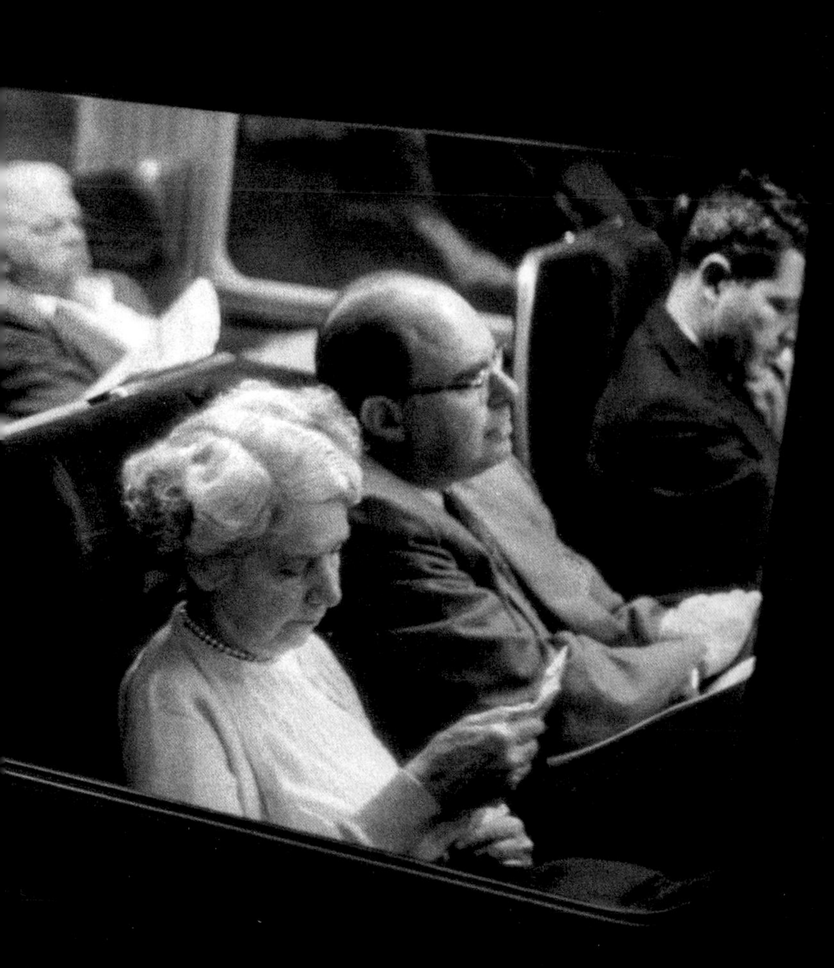

27. Penn Station, New York, 1958.

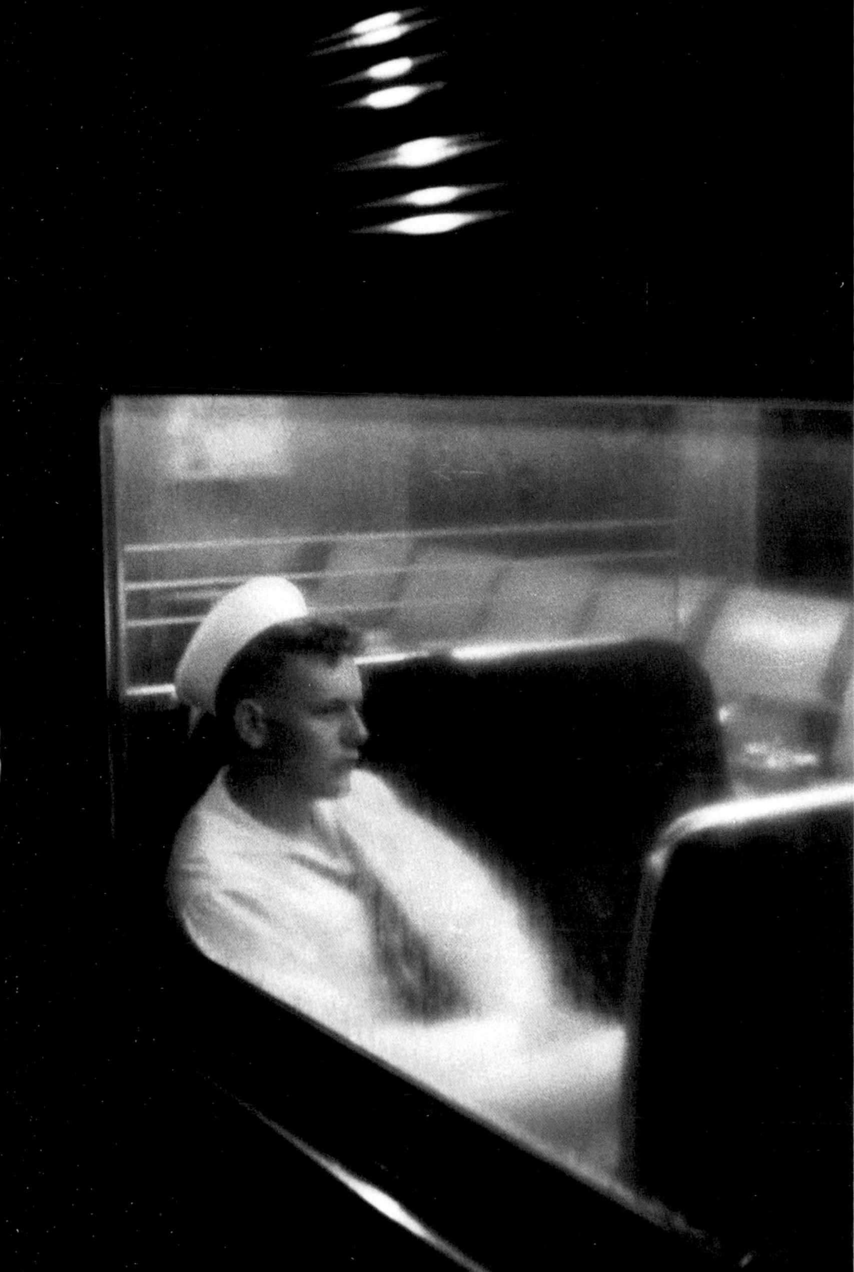

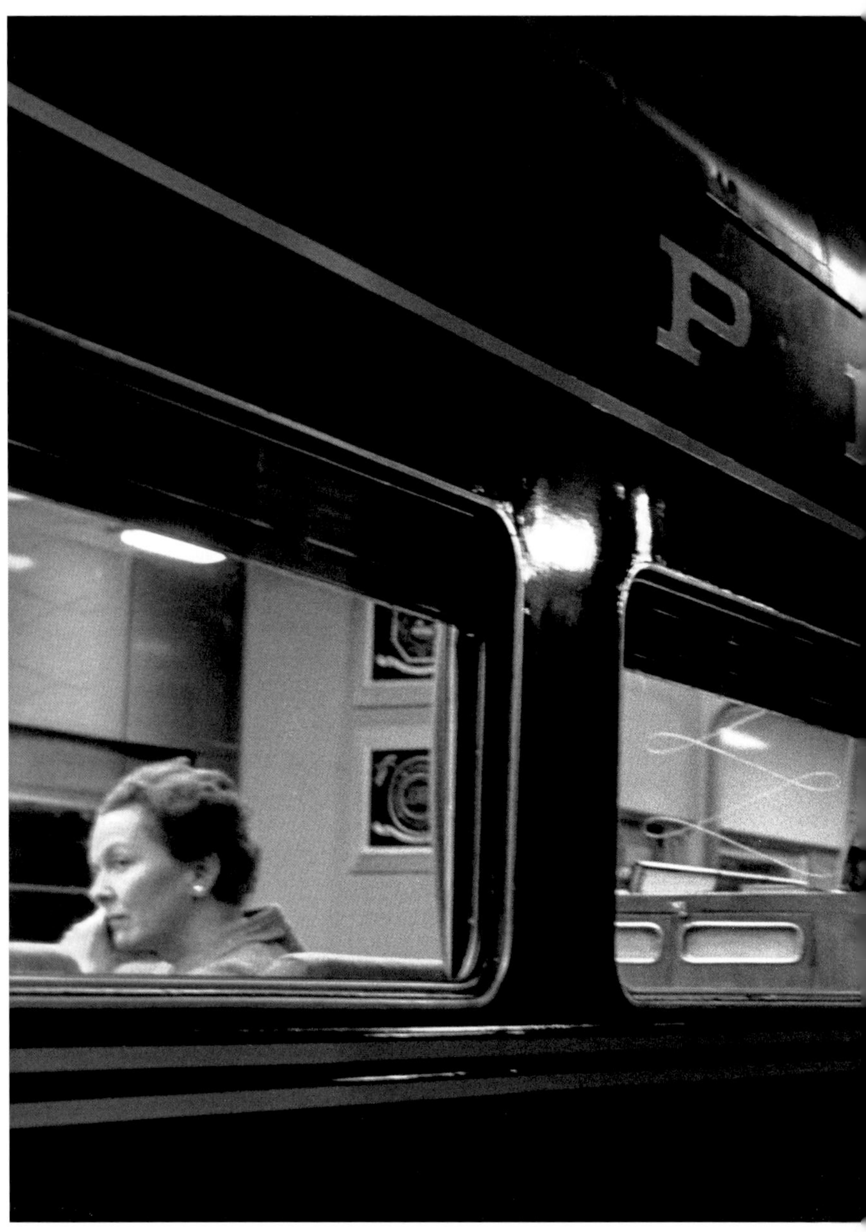

28. Penn Station, New York, 1958.

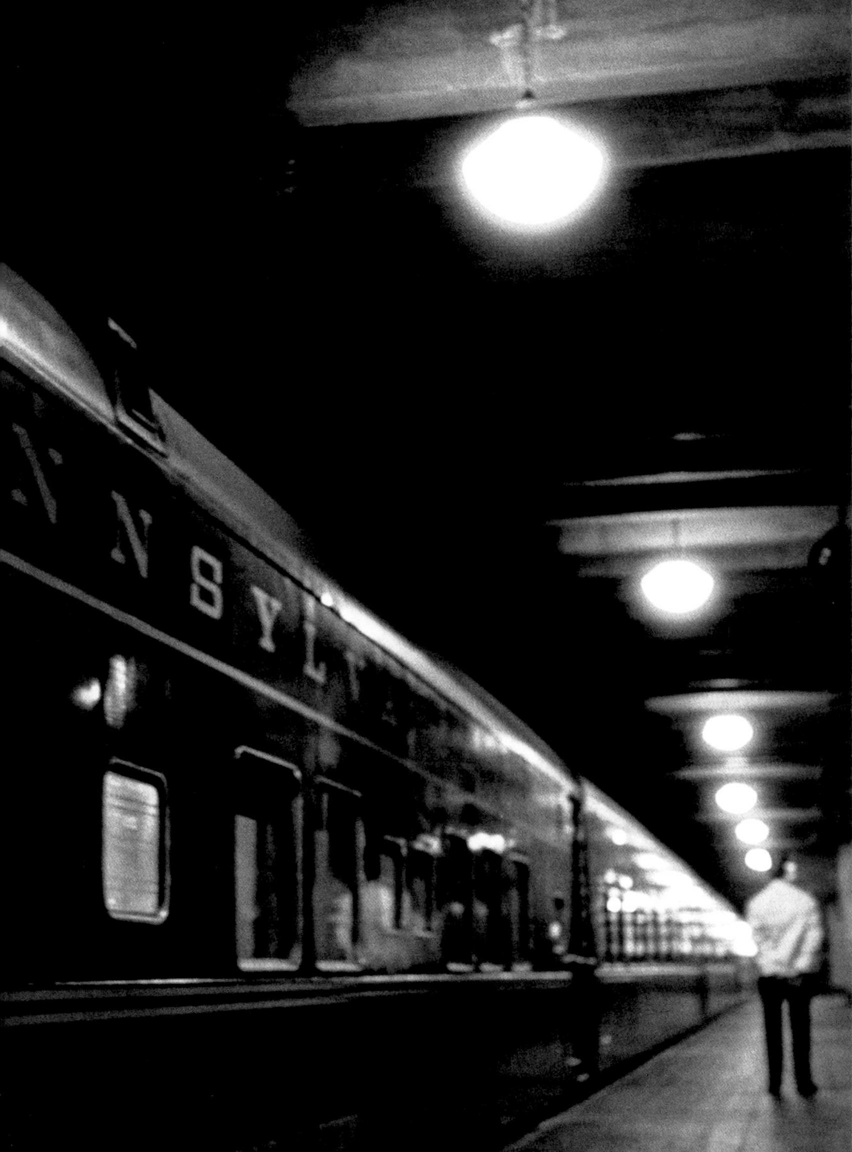
NSYL

29. Penn Station, New York, 1958.

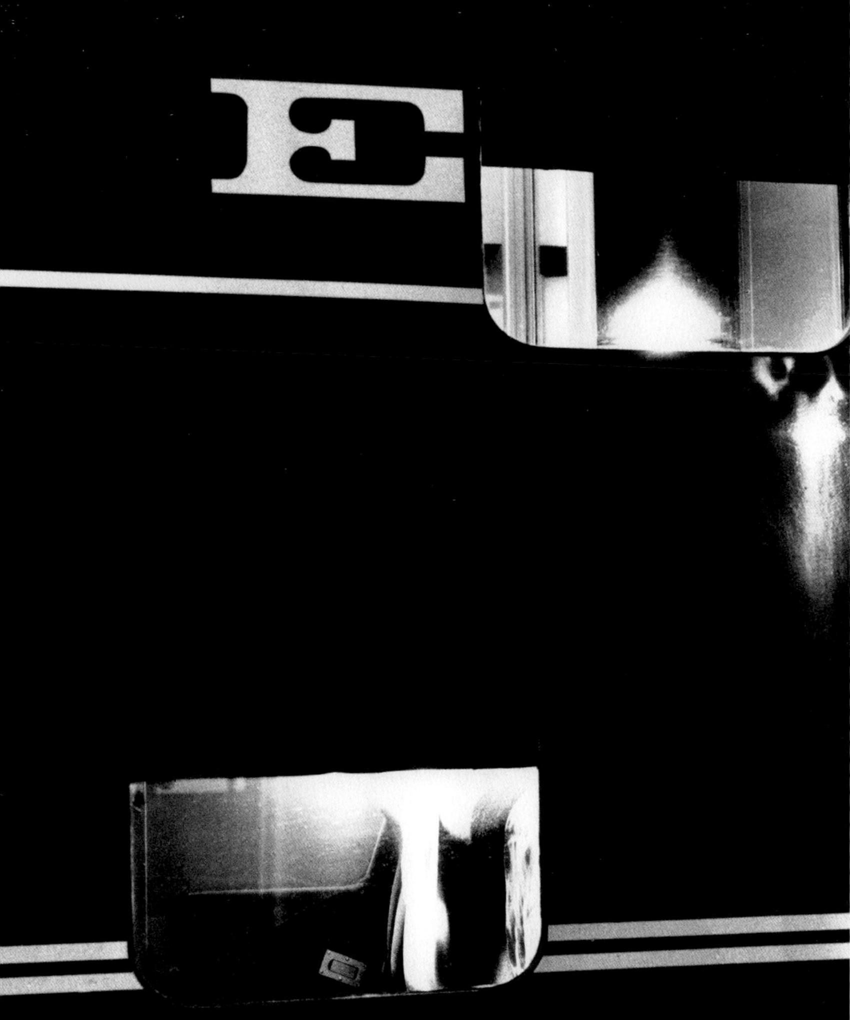

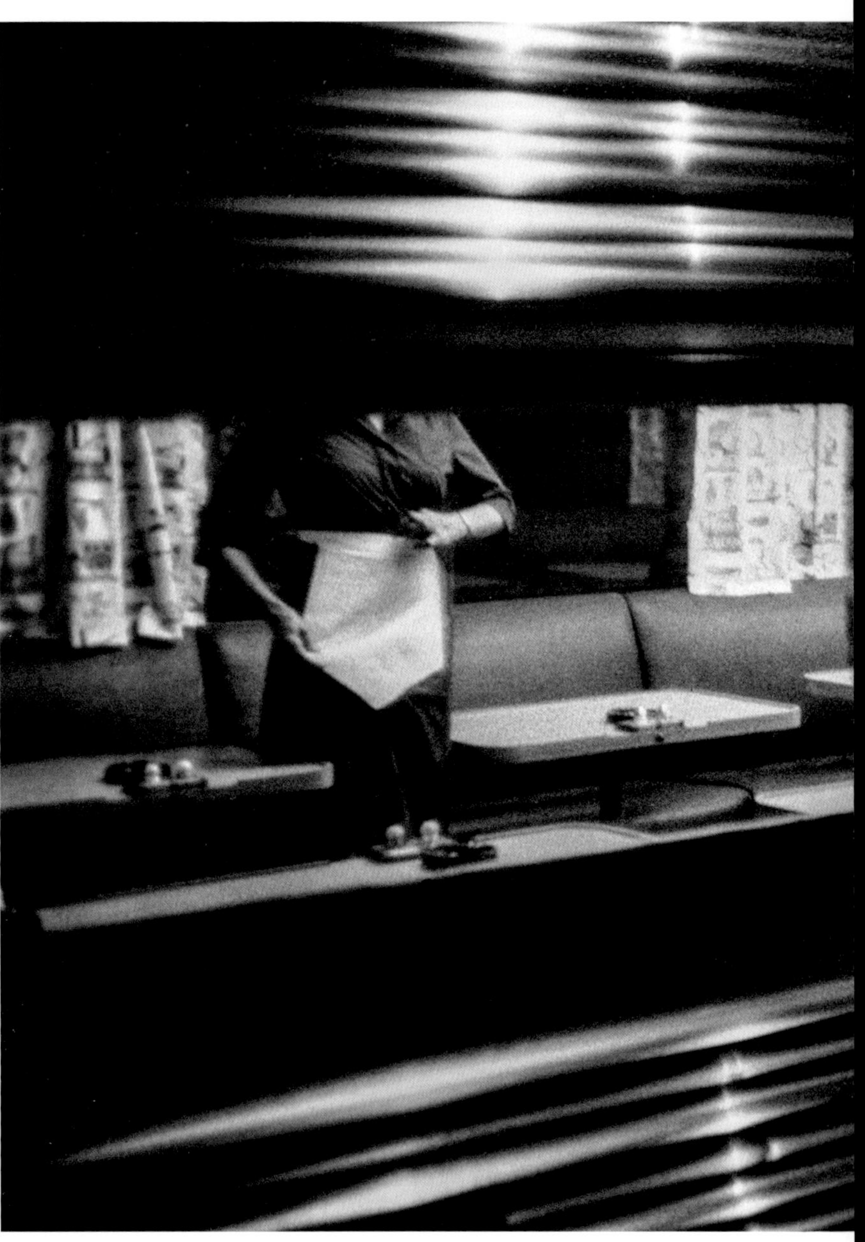

30. Penn Station, New York, 1958.

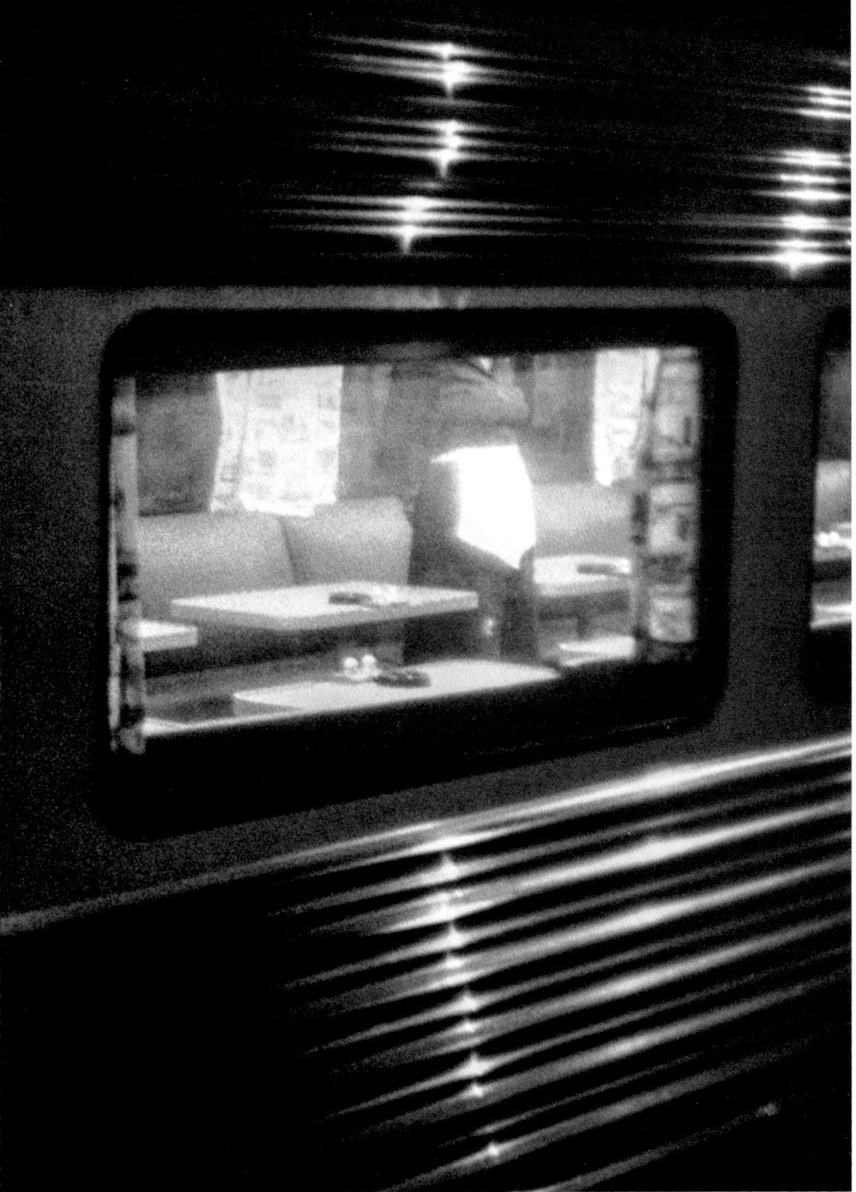

31. Penn Station, New York, 1958.

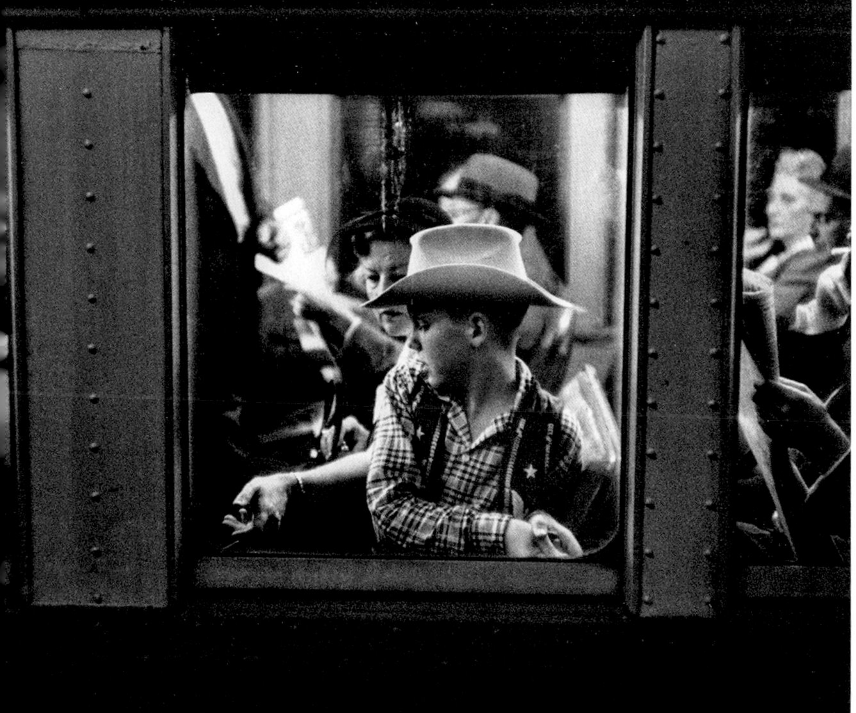

32. Penn Station, New York, 1958.

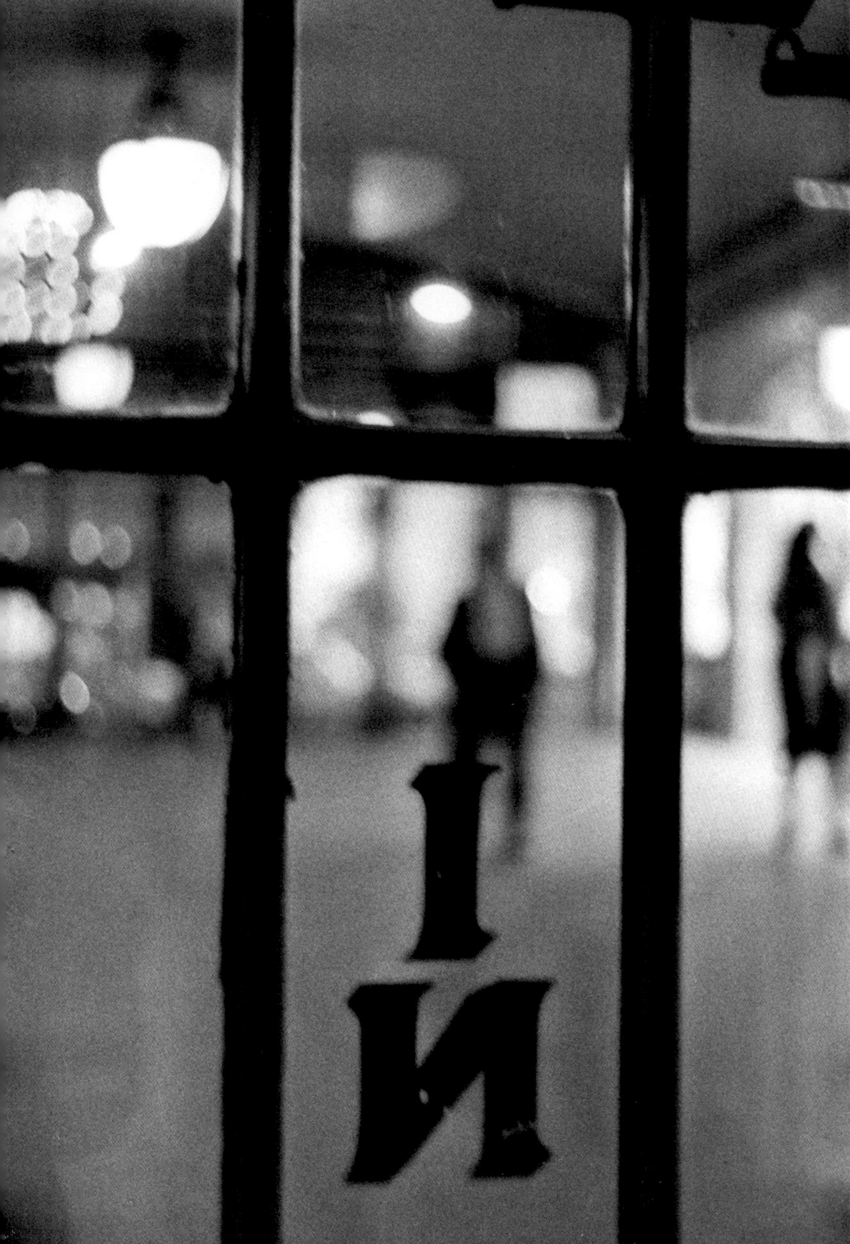

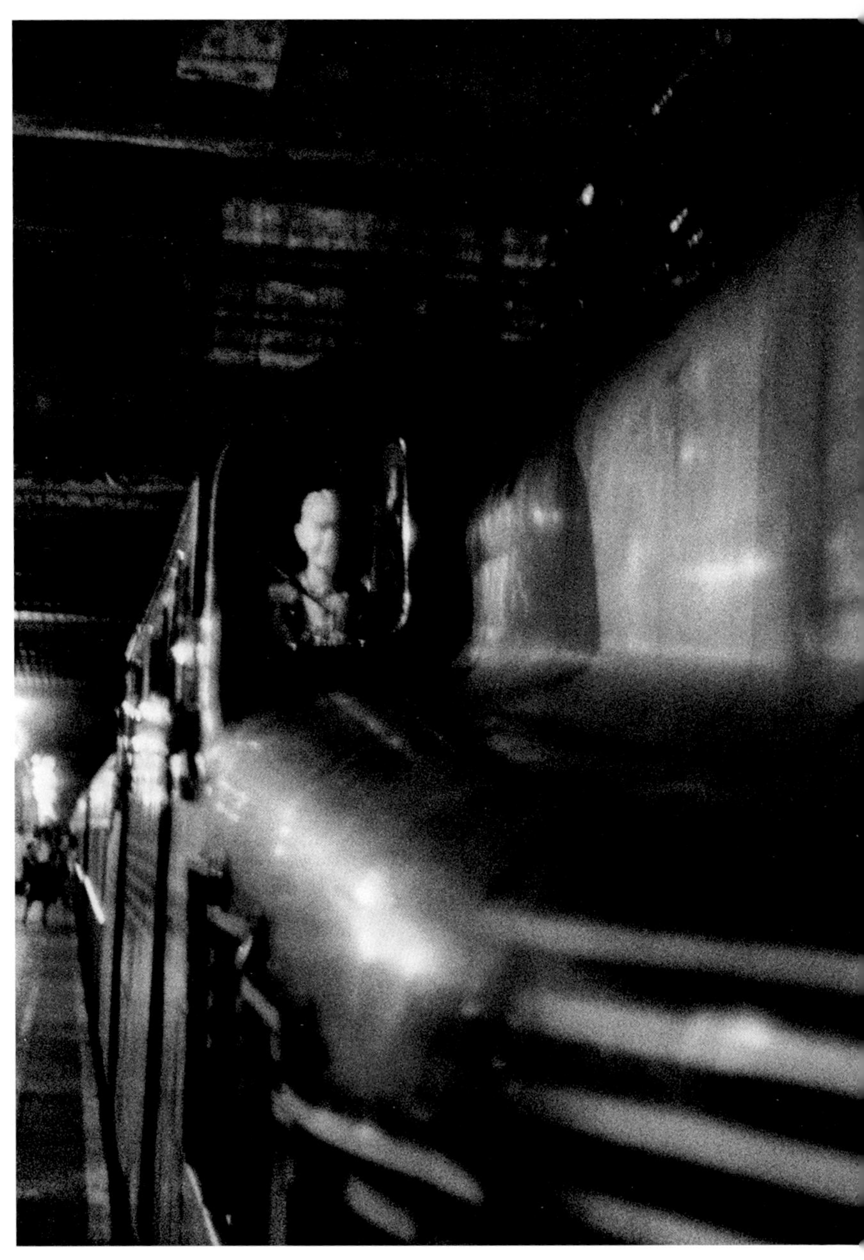

33. Penn Station, New York, 1958.

34. Penn Station, New York, 1958.

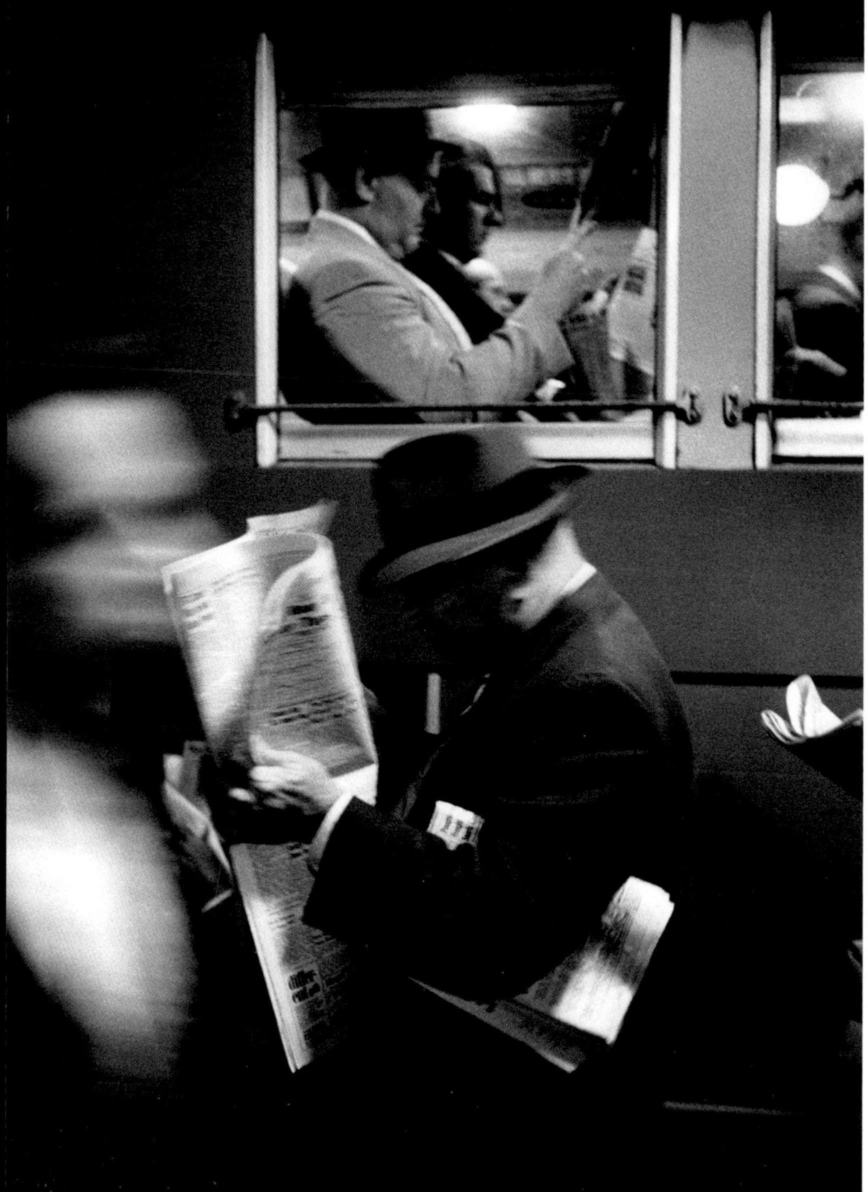

35. Penn Station, New York, 1958.

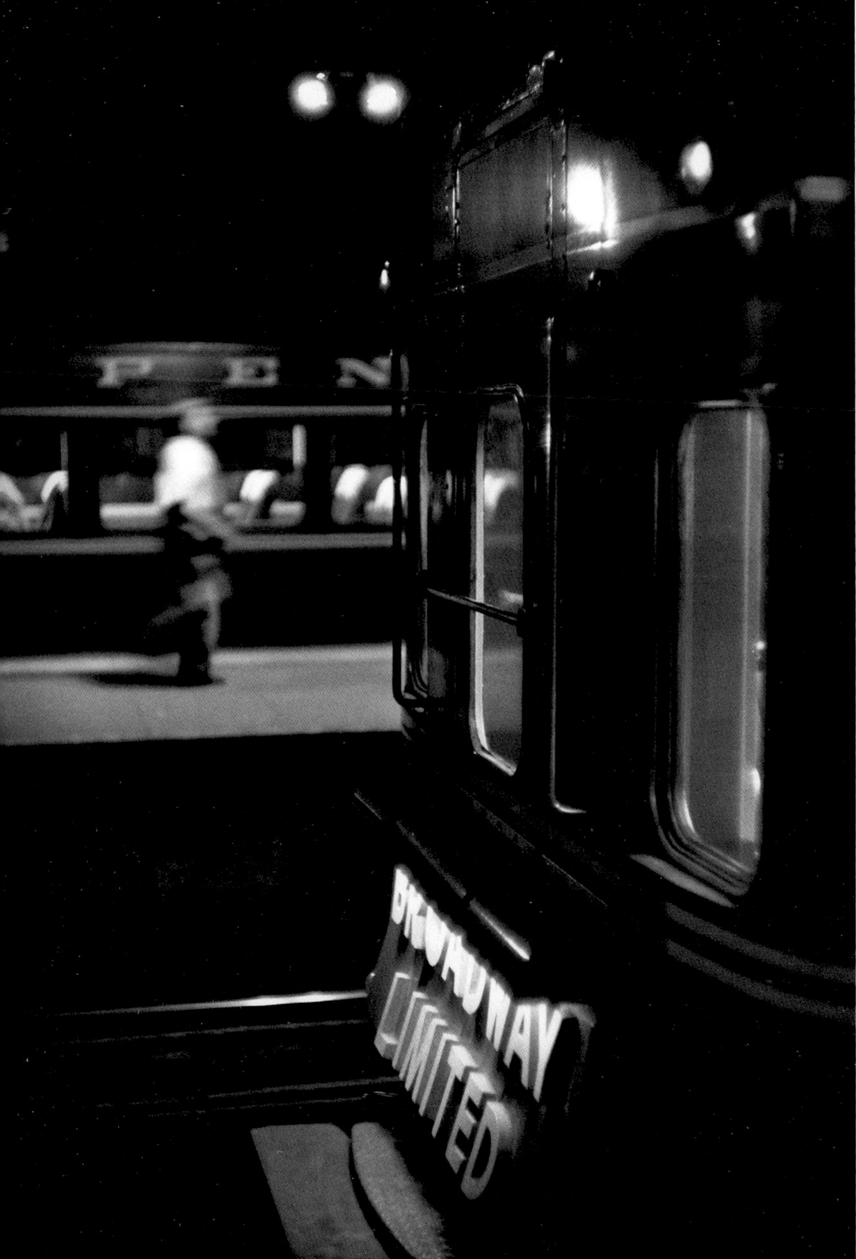
PENN
BROADWAY
LIMITED

36. Penn Station, New York, 1958.

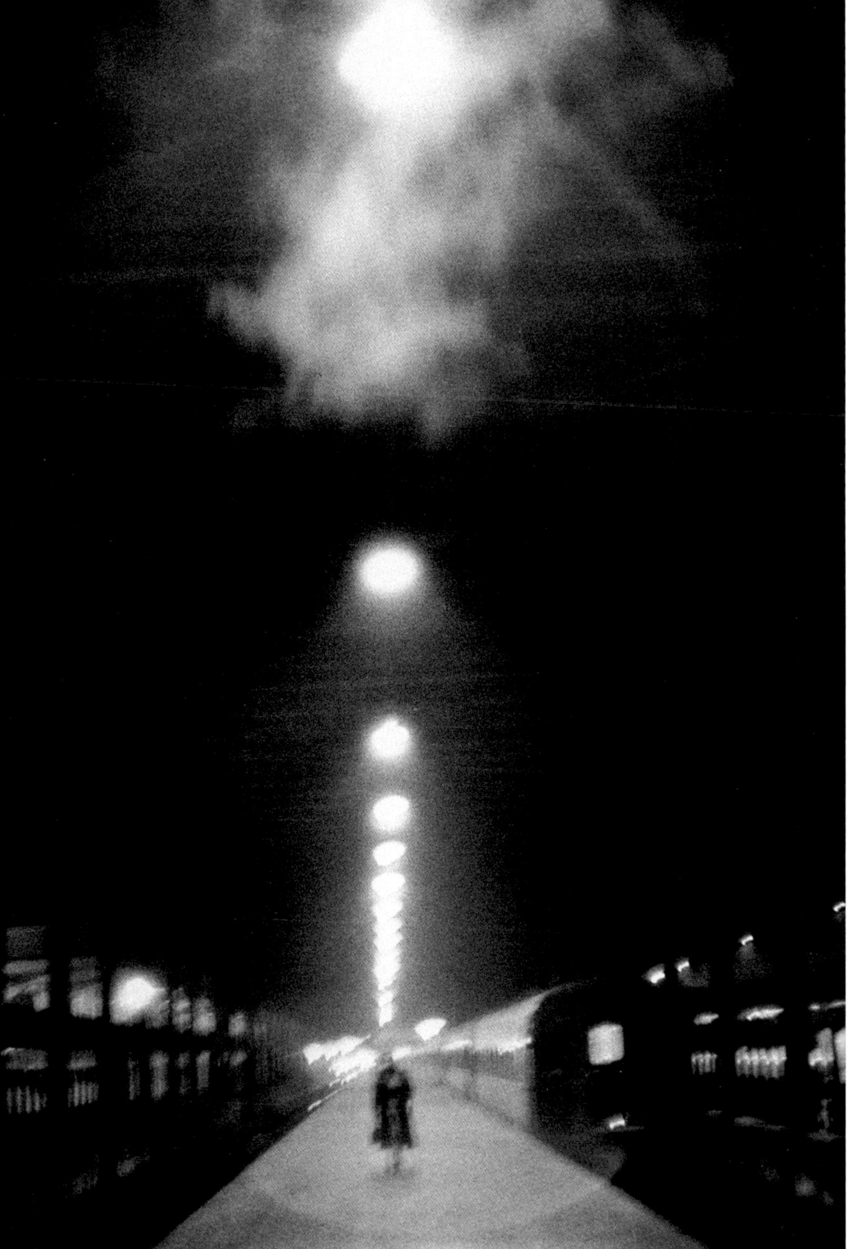

37. Nancy listening to jazz, Greenwich Village, New York, 1958.

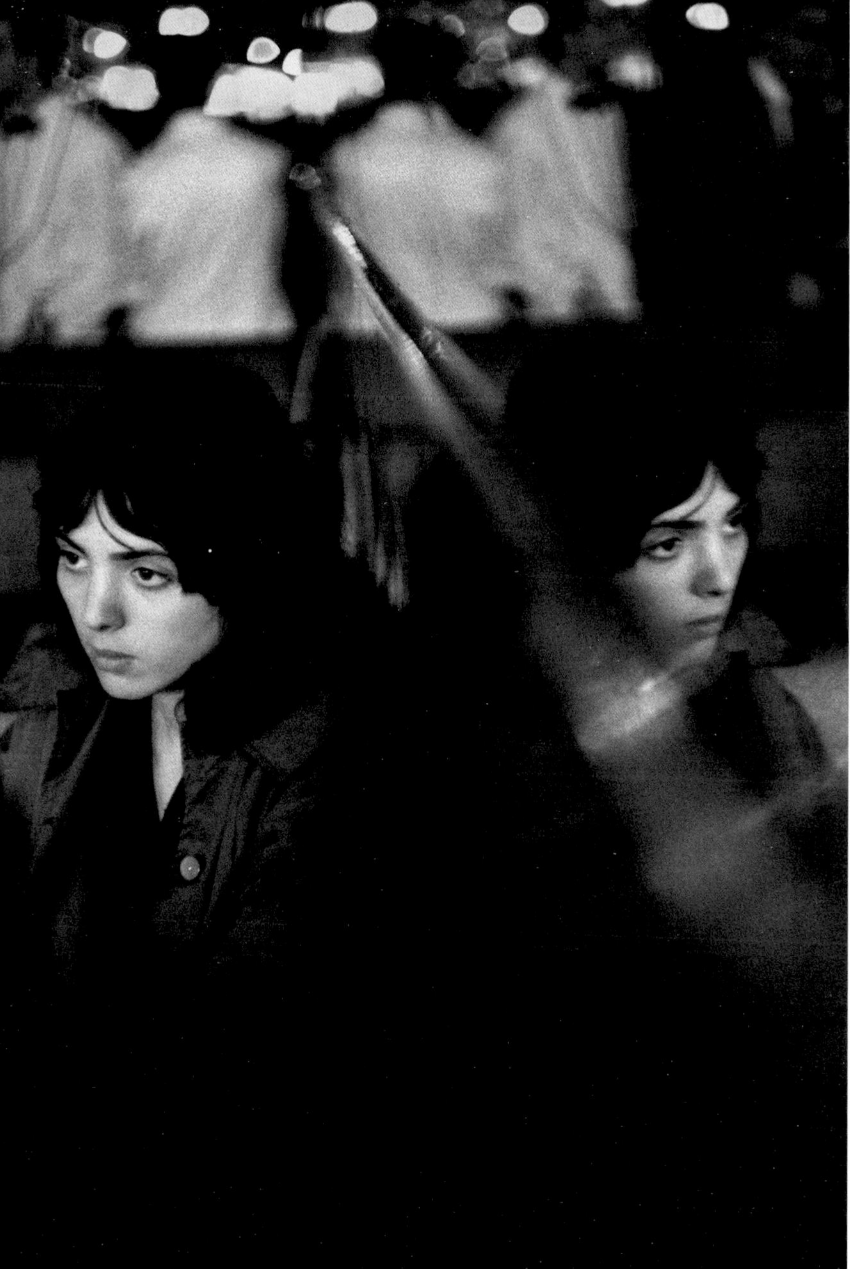

38. Nancy playing with cup, New York, 1958.

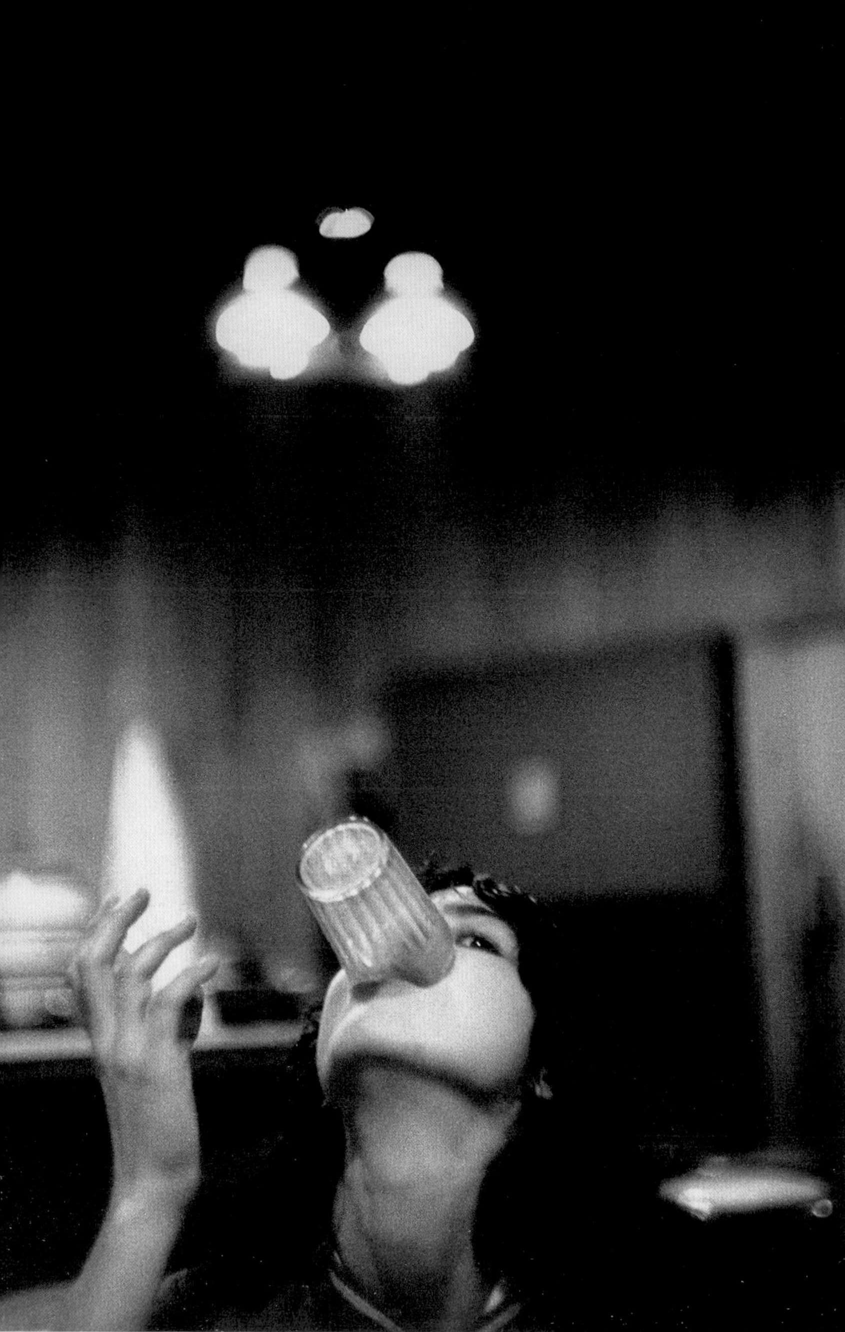

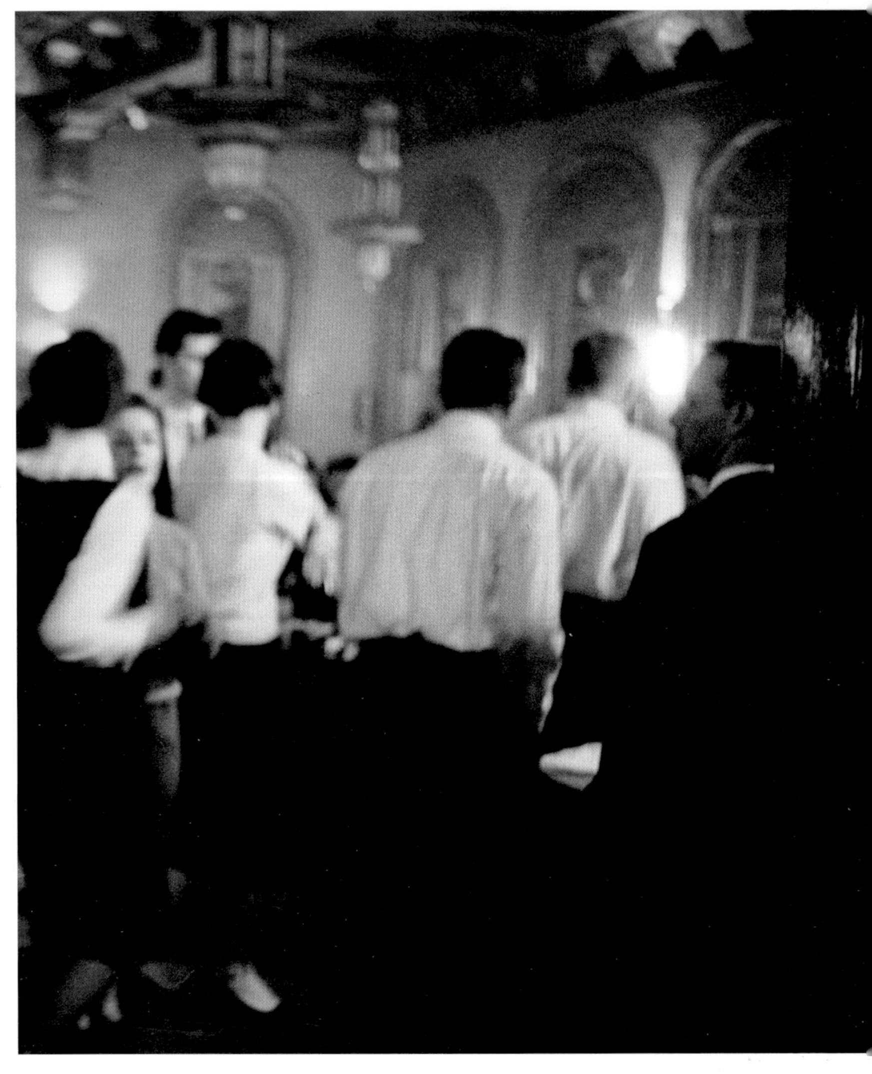

39. Nancy listening to jazz, New York, 1958.

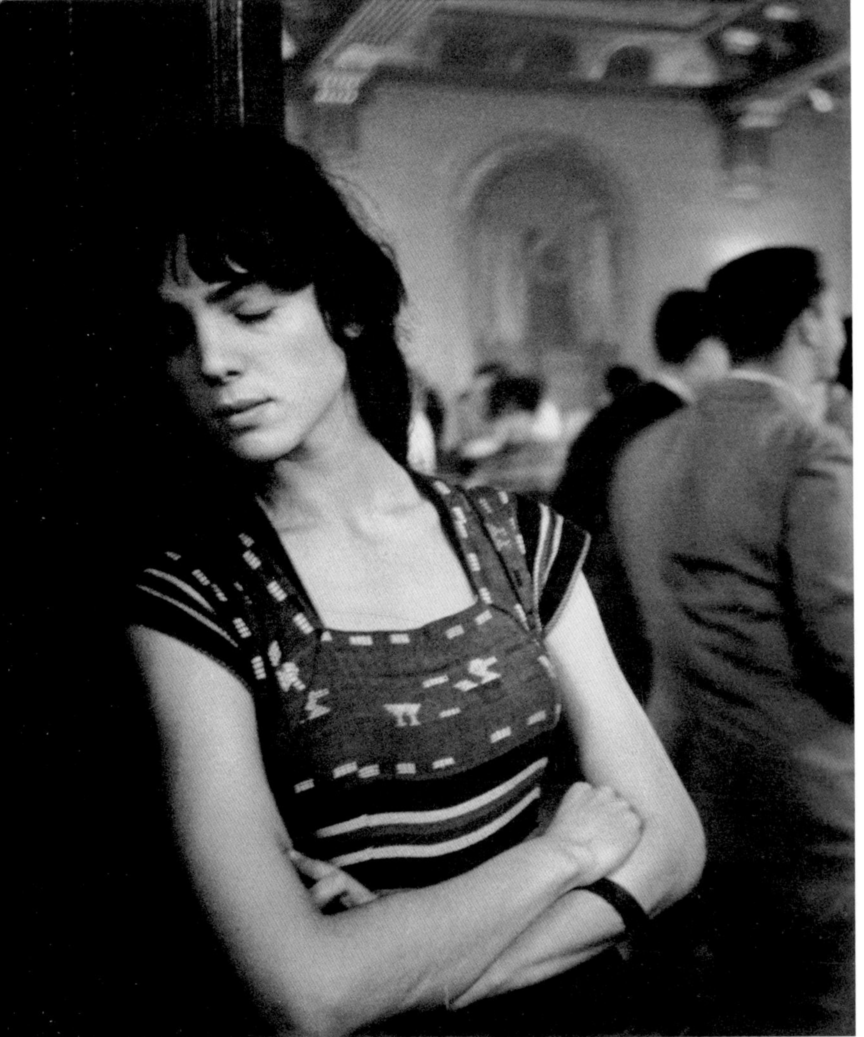

40. Nancy on the bus, New York, 1958.

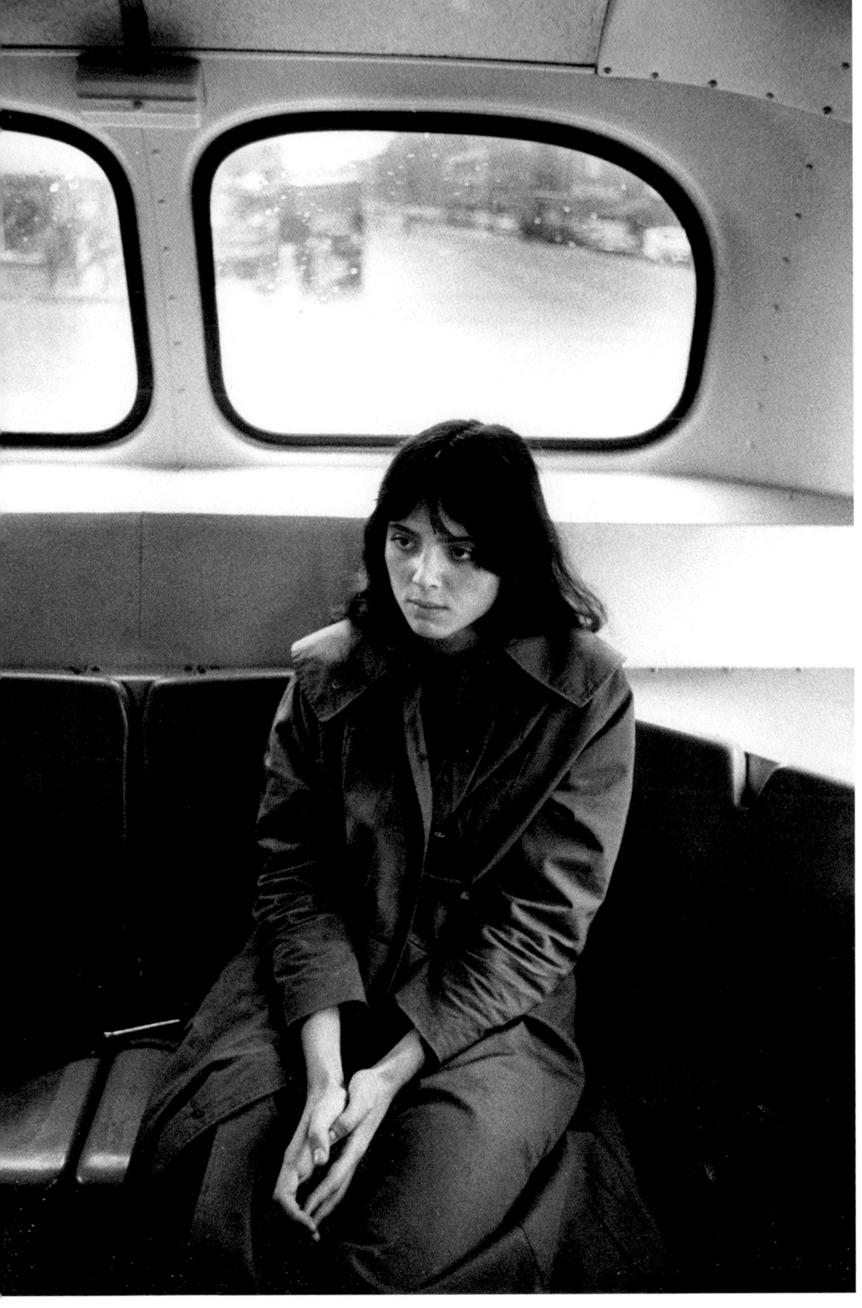

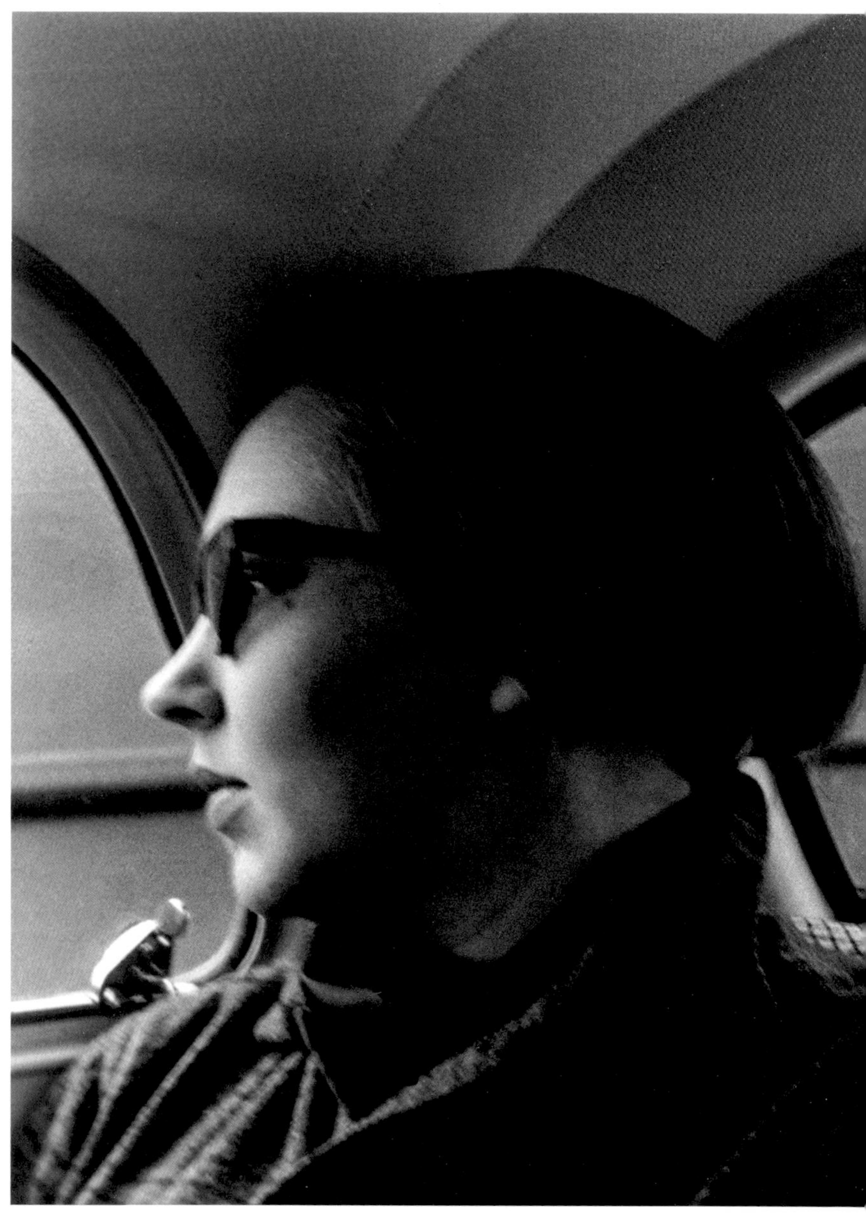

41. On the ferry, the Netherlands, 1962.

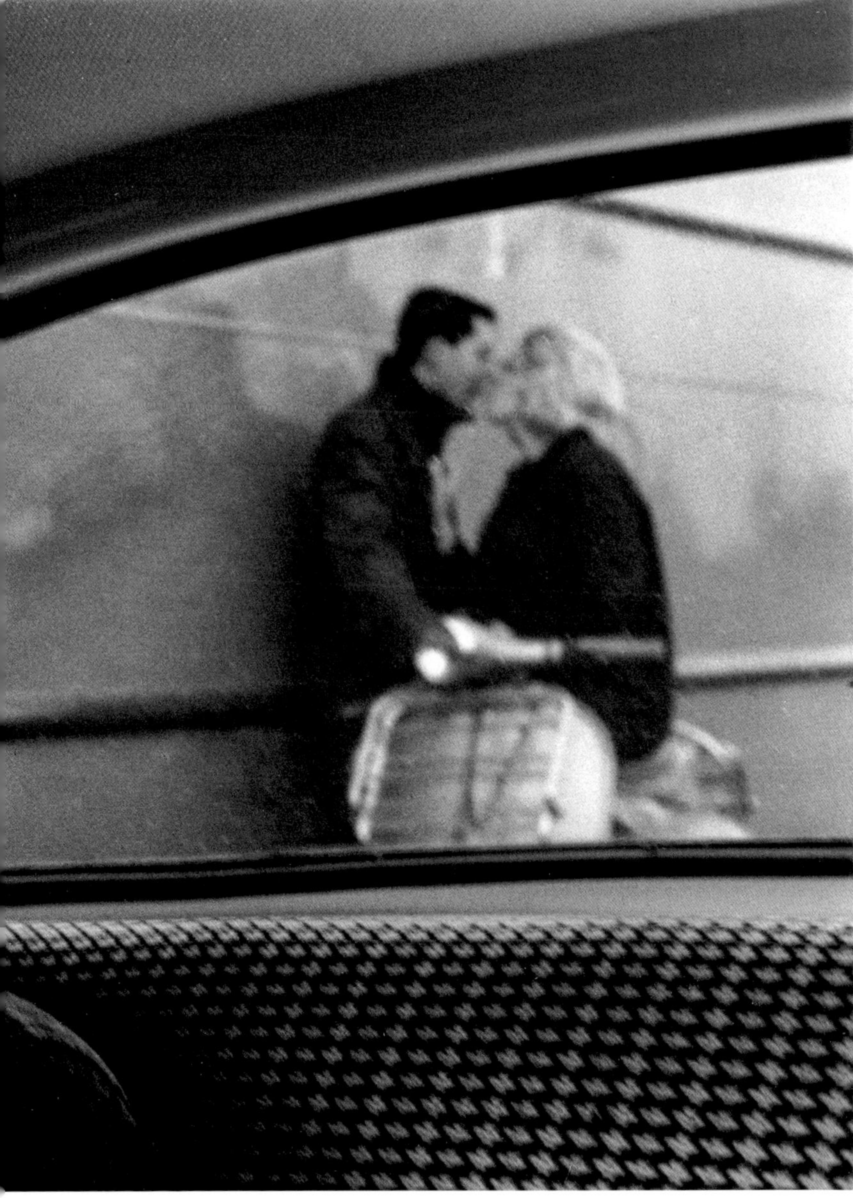

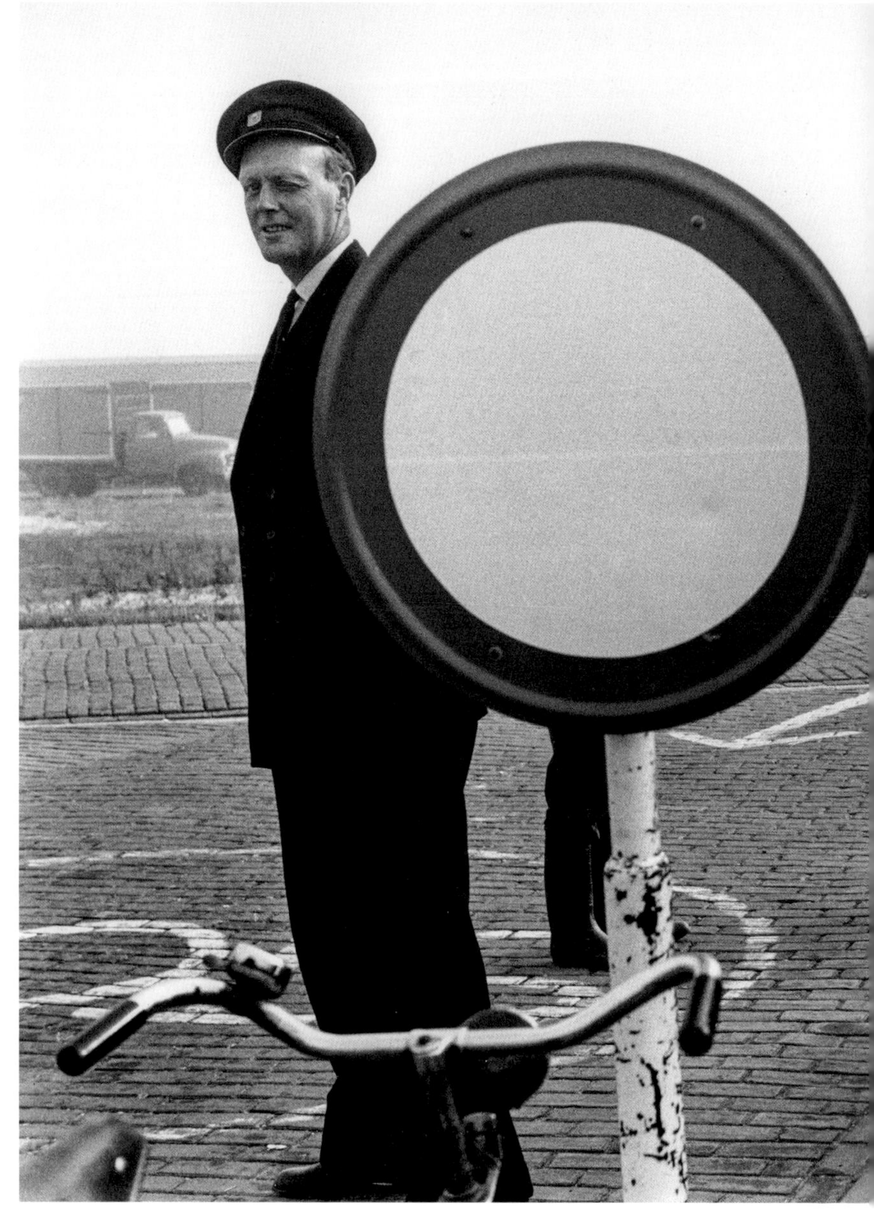

42. Parking lot, Volendam, the Netherlands, 1962.

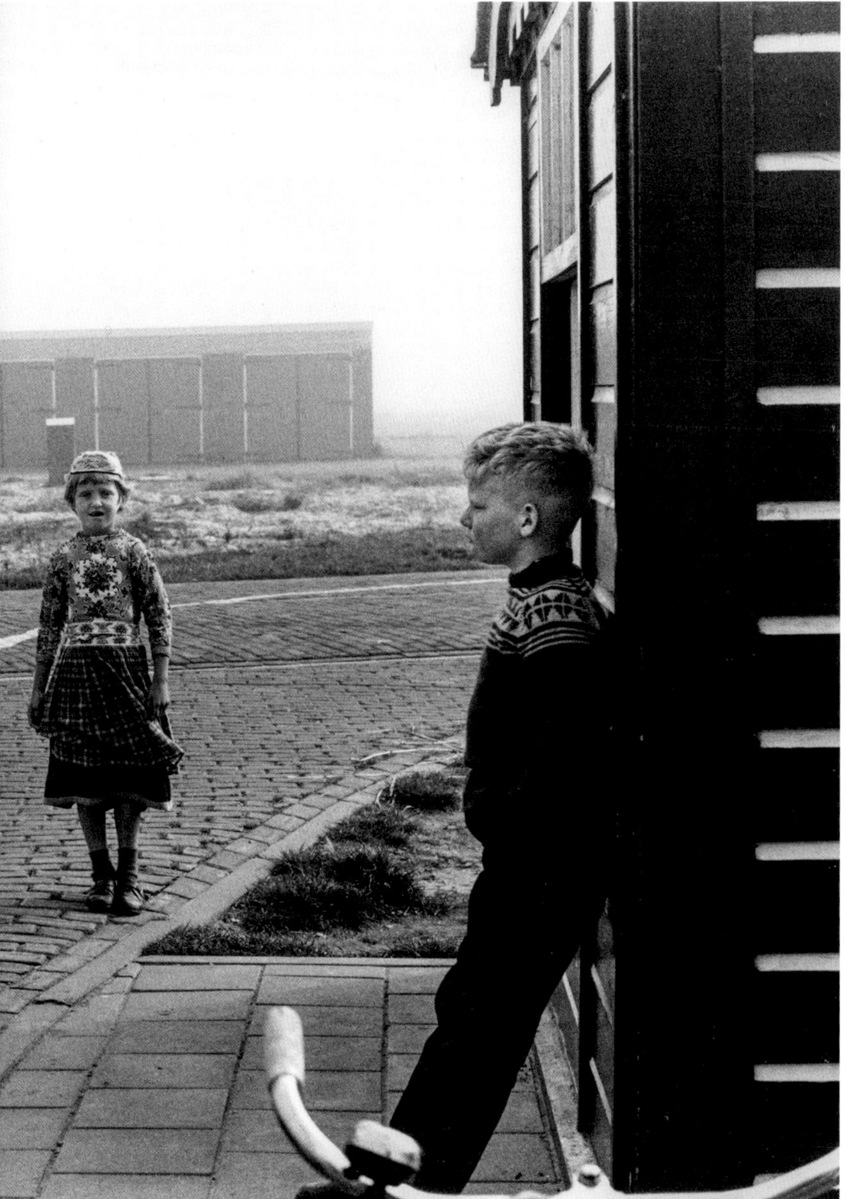

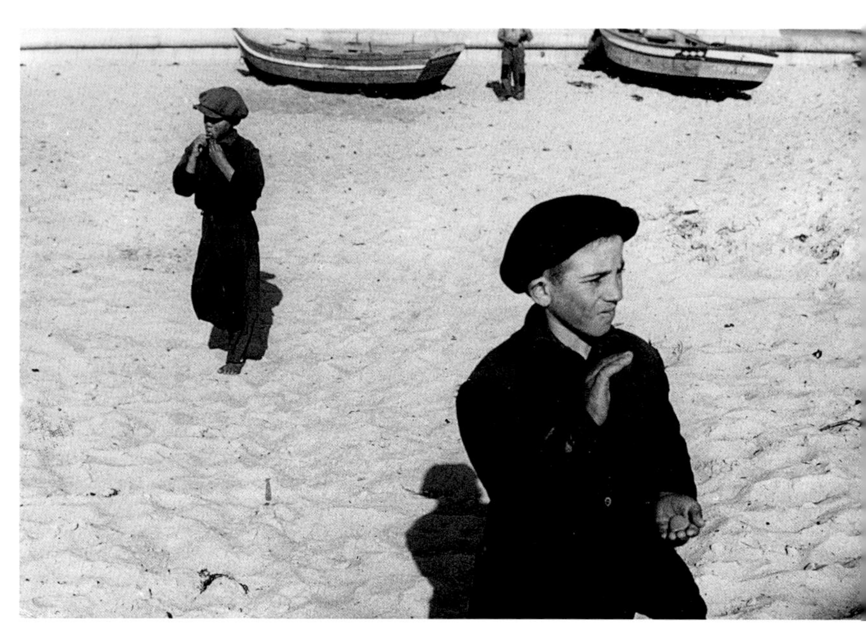

43. Fishermen's children, Nazaré, Portugal, ca. 1959.
44. Children playing, Provincetown, Massachusetts, ca. 1952–1954.

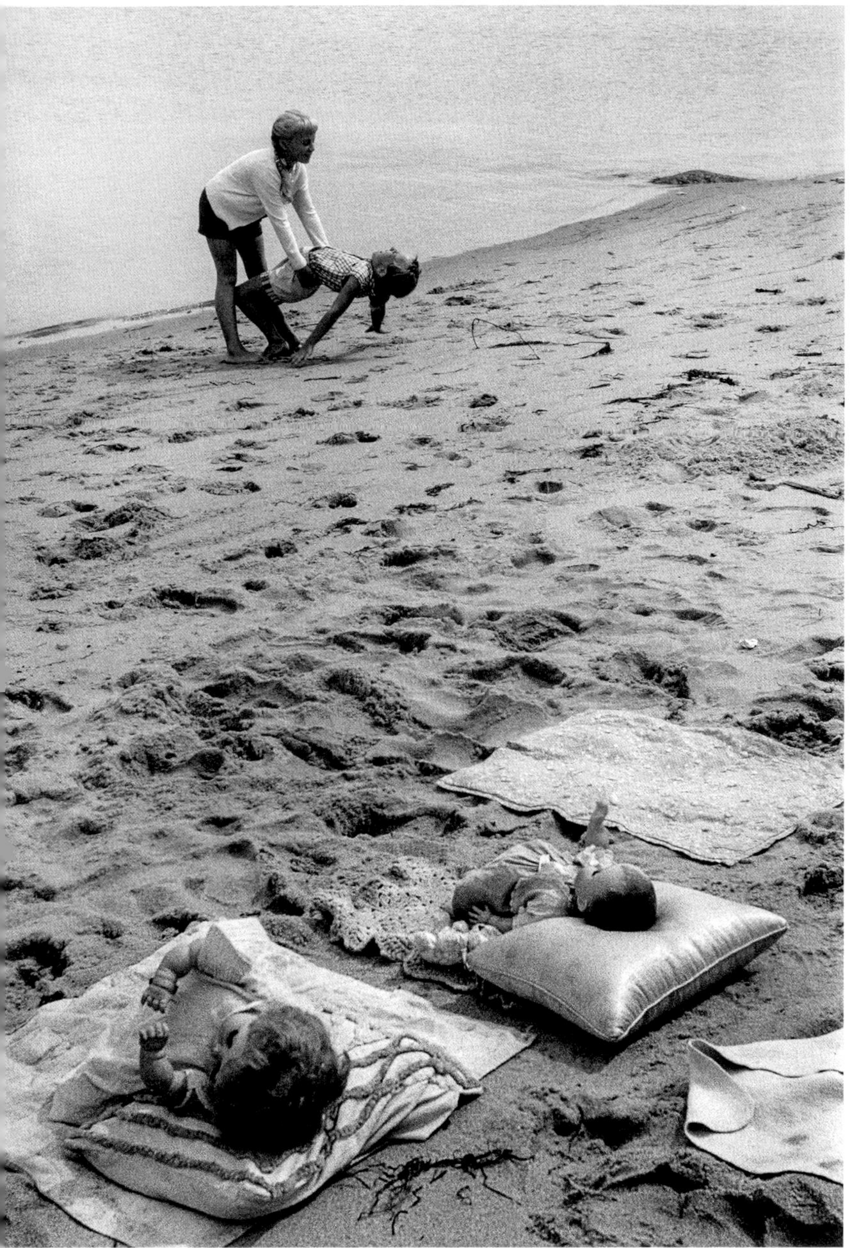

45. Saint-Raphaël, ca. 1958–1960.

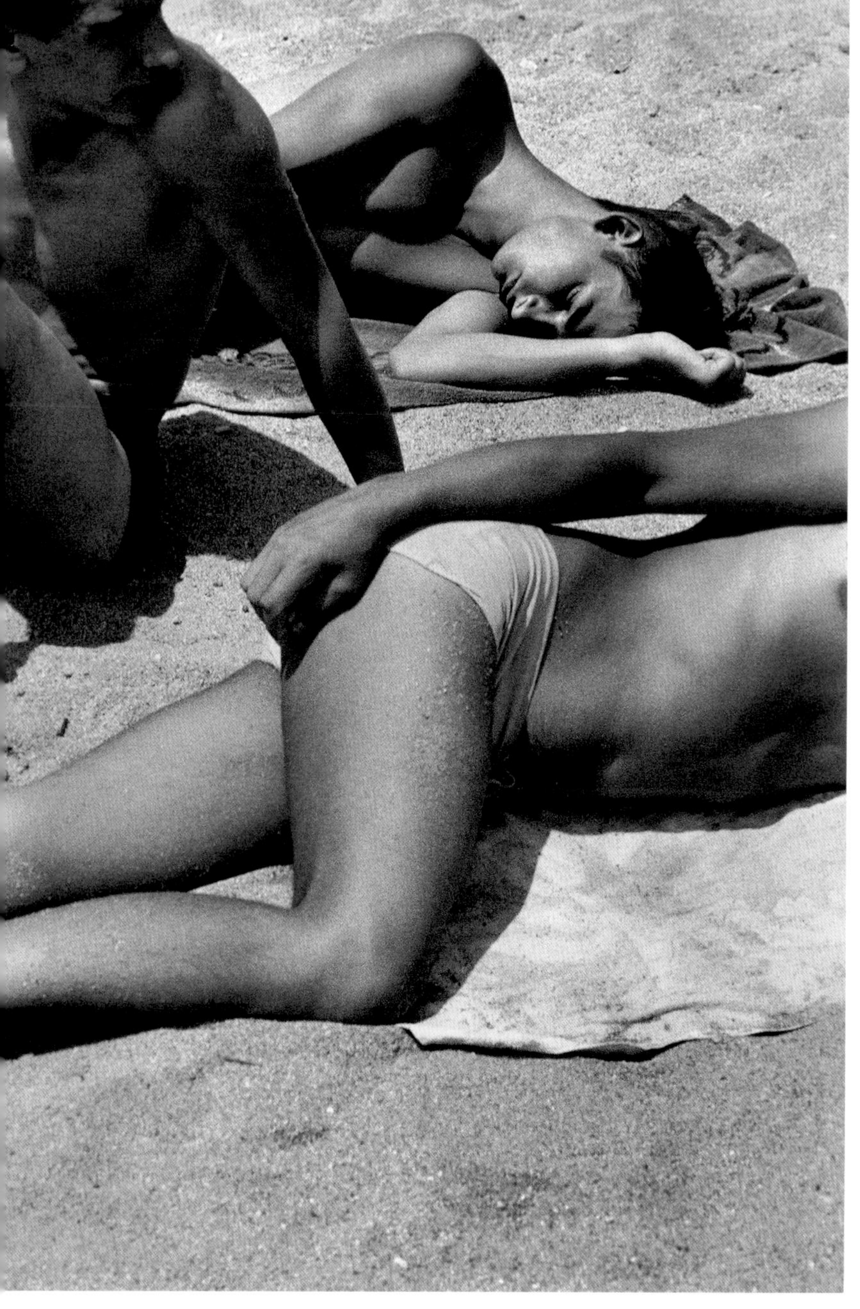

46. Tony, Fisherman, Ibiza, ca. 1960–1962.

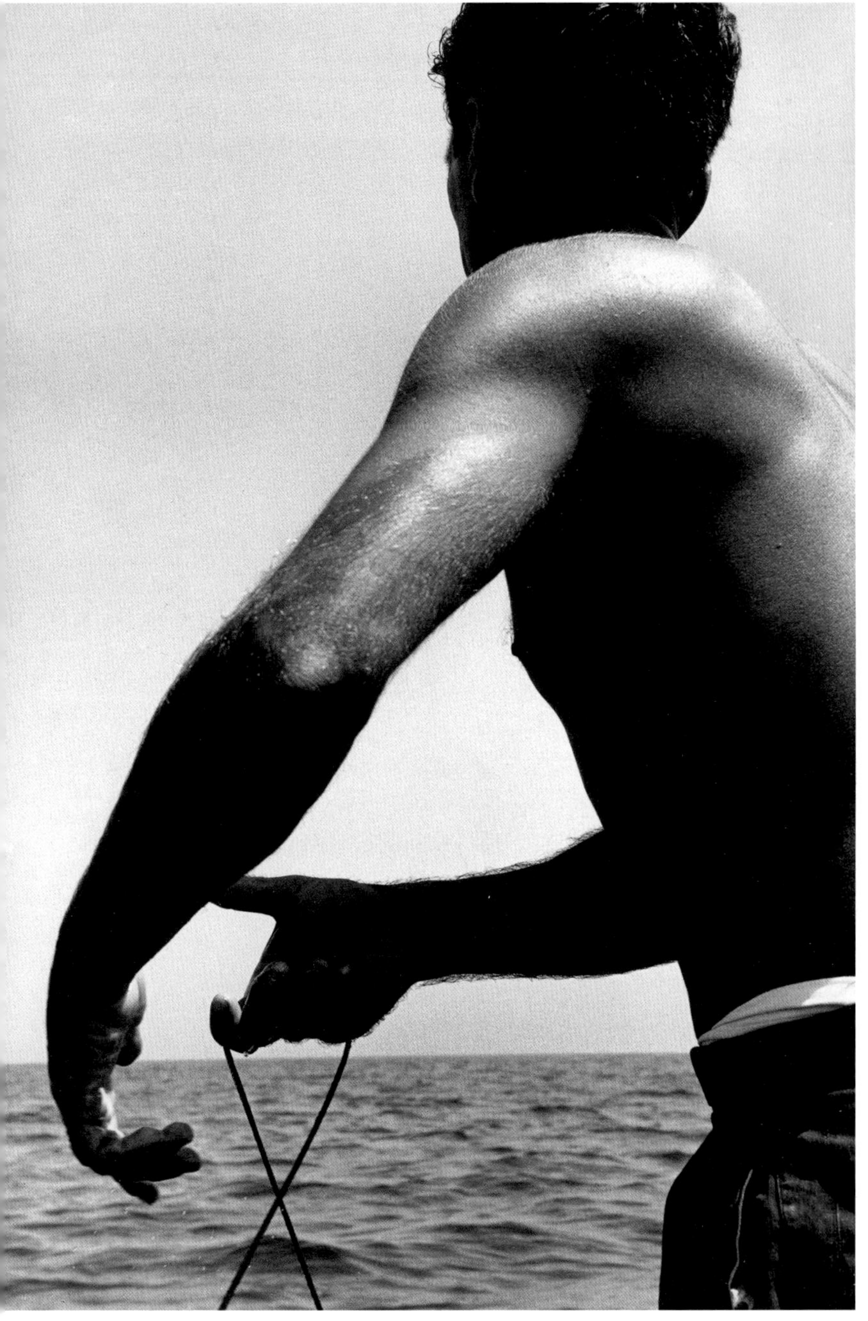

47. Mexico, ca. 1956.

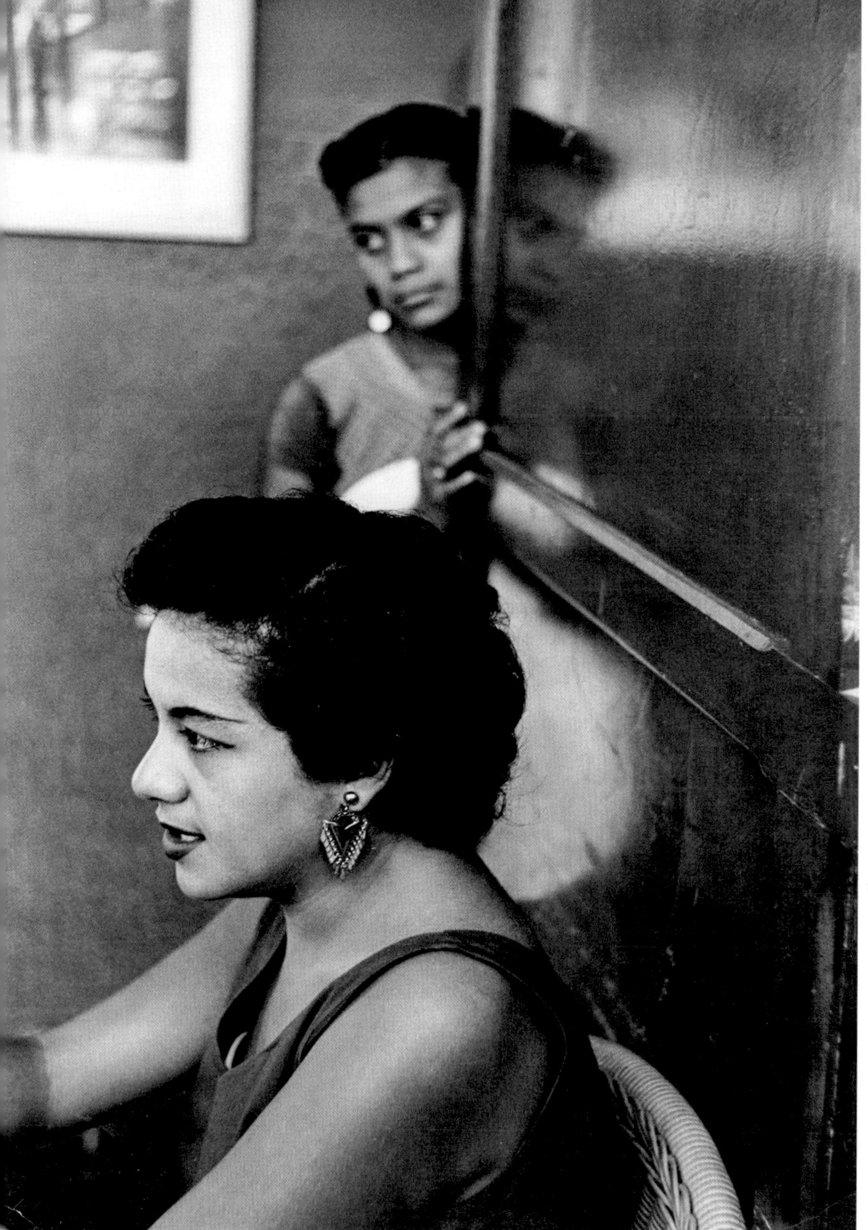

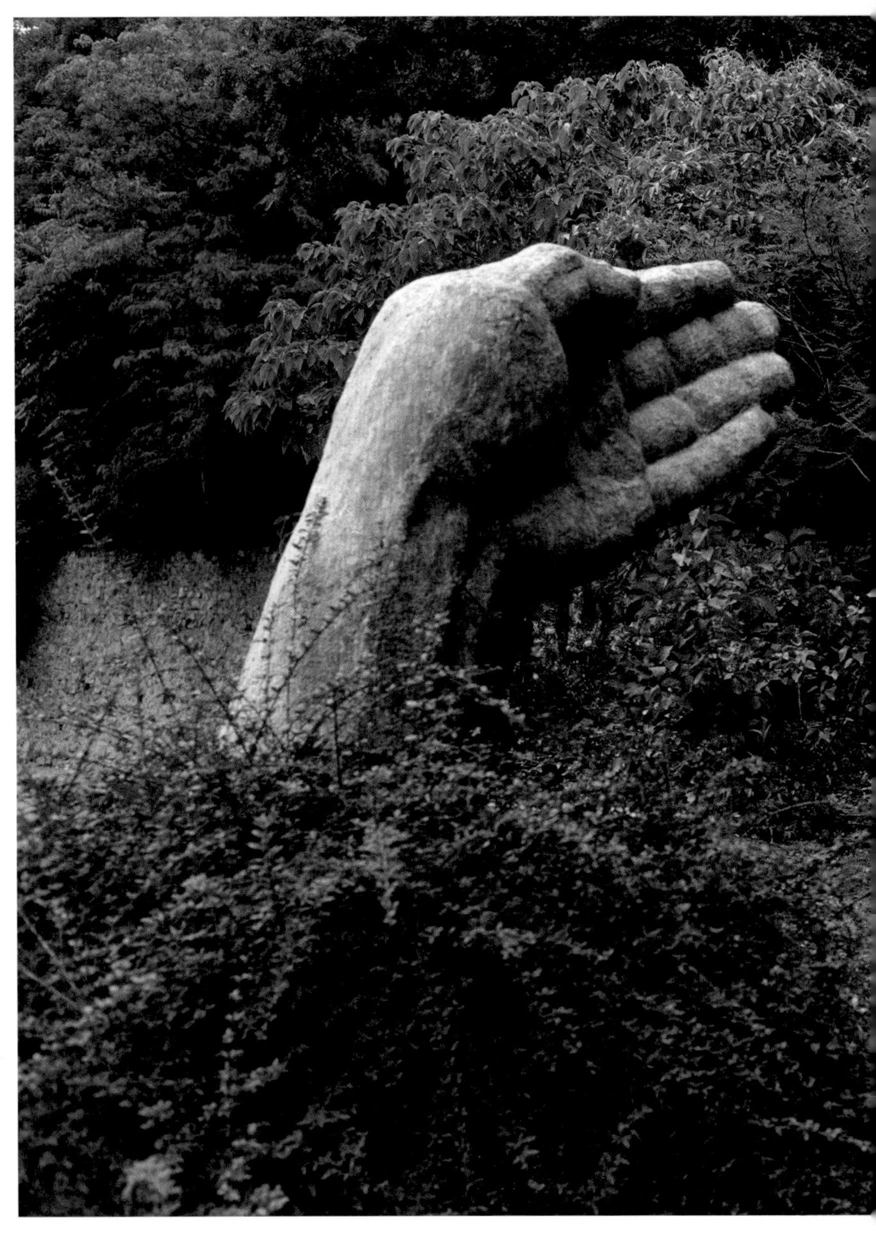

48. Soviet Union, 1975.

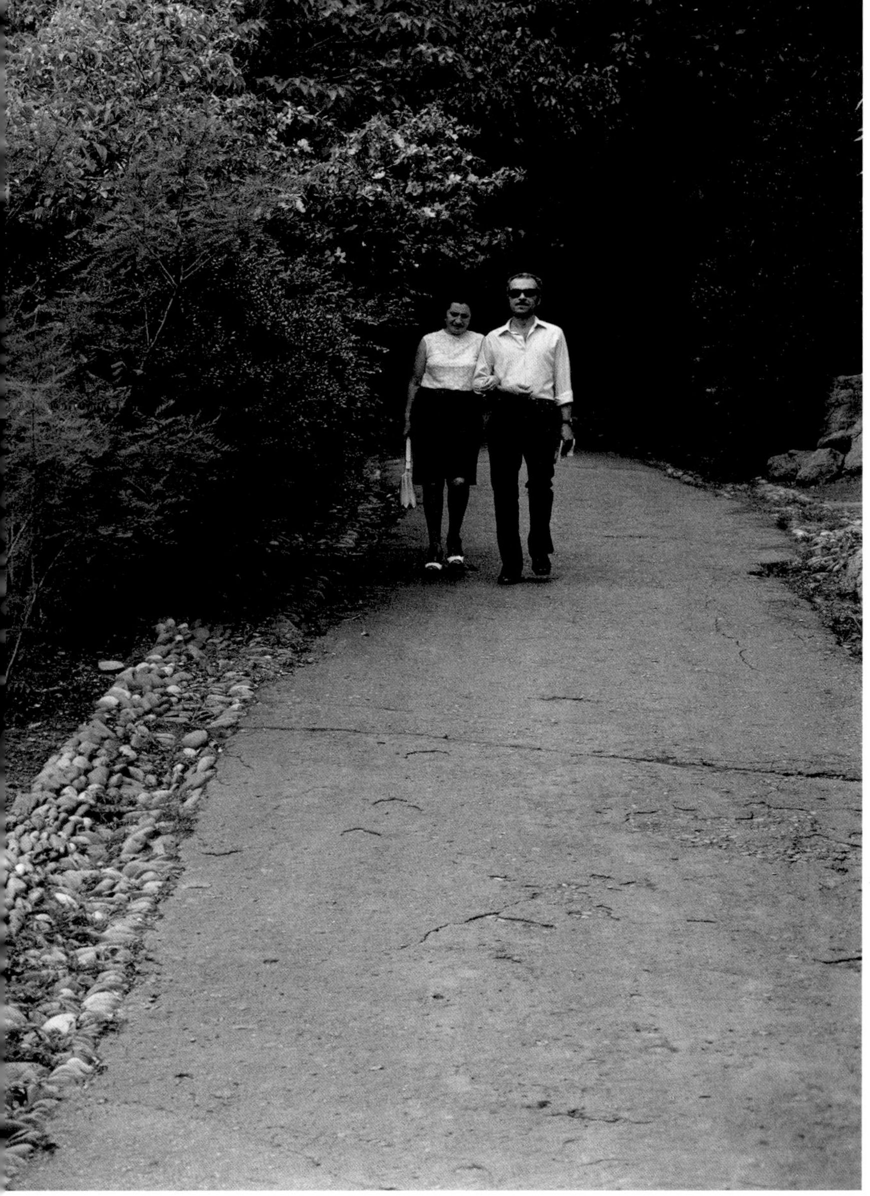

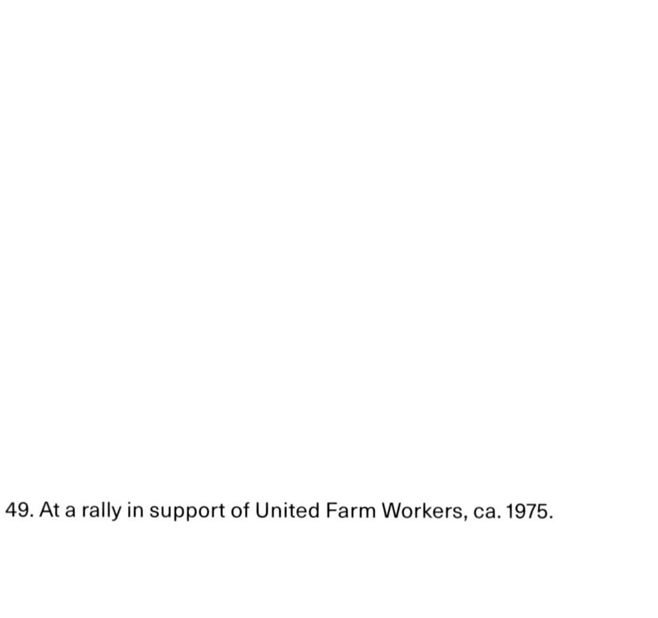

49. At a rally in support of United Farm Workers, ca. 1975.

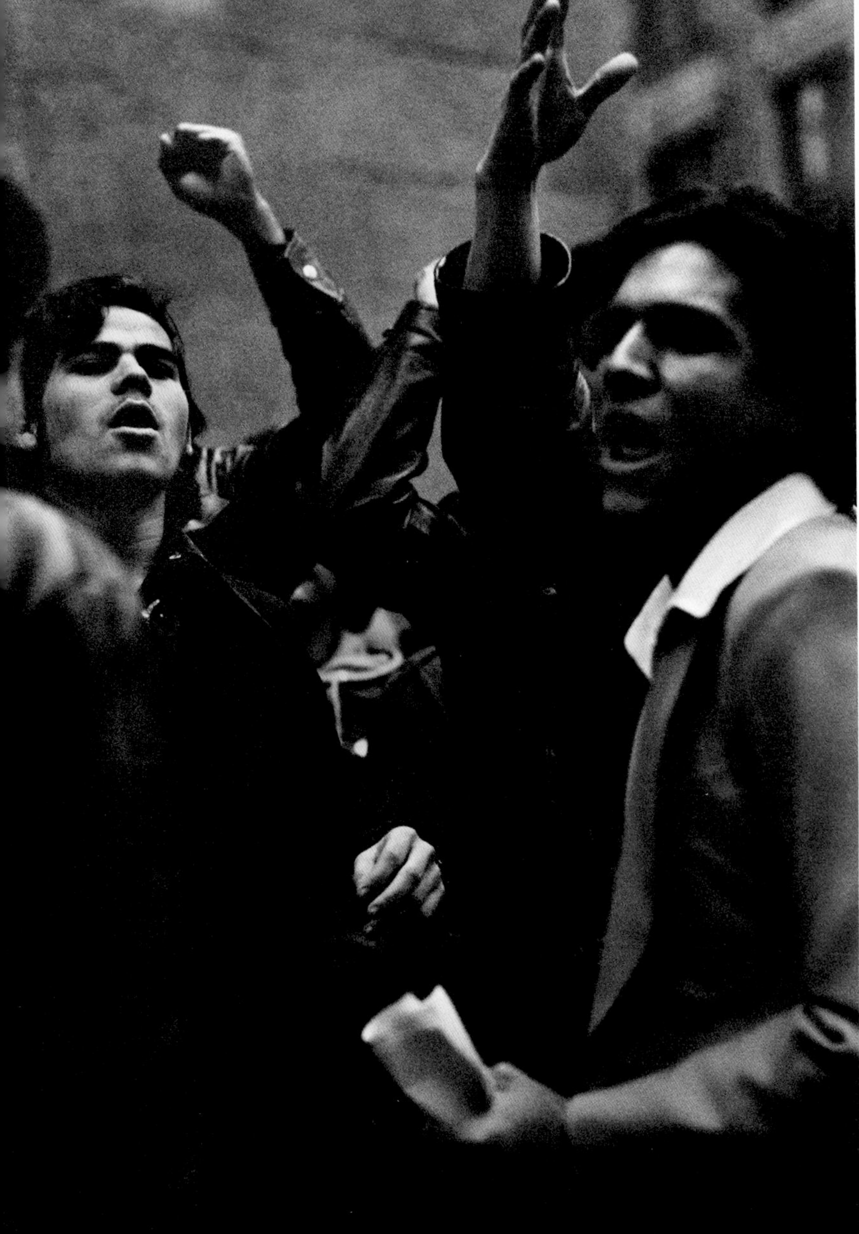

50. At a rally in support of United Farm Workers, ca. 1975.

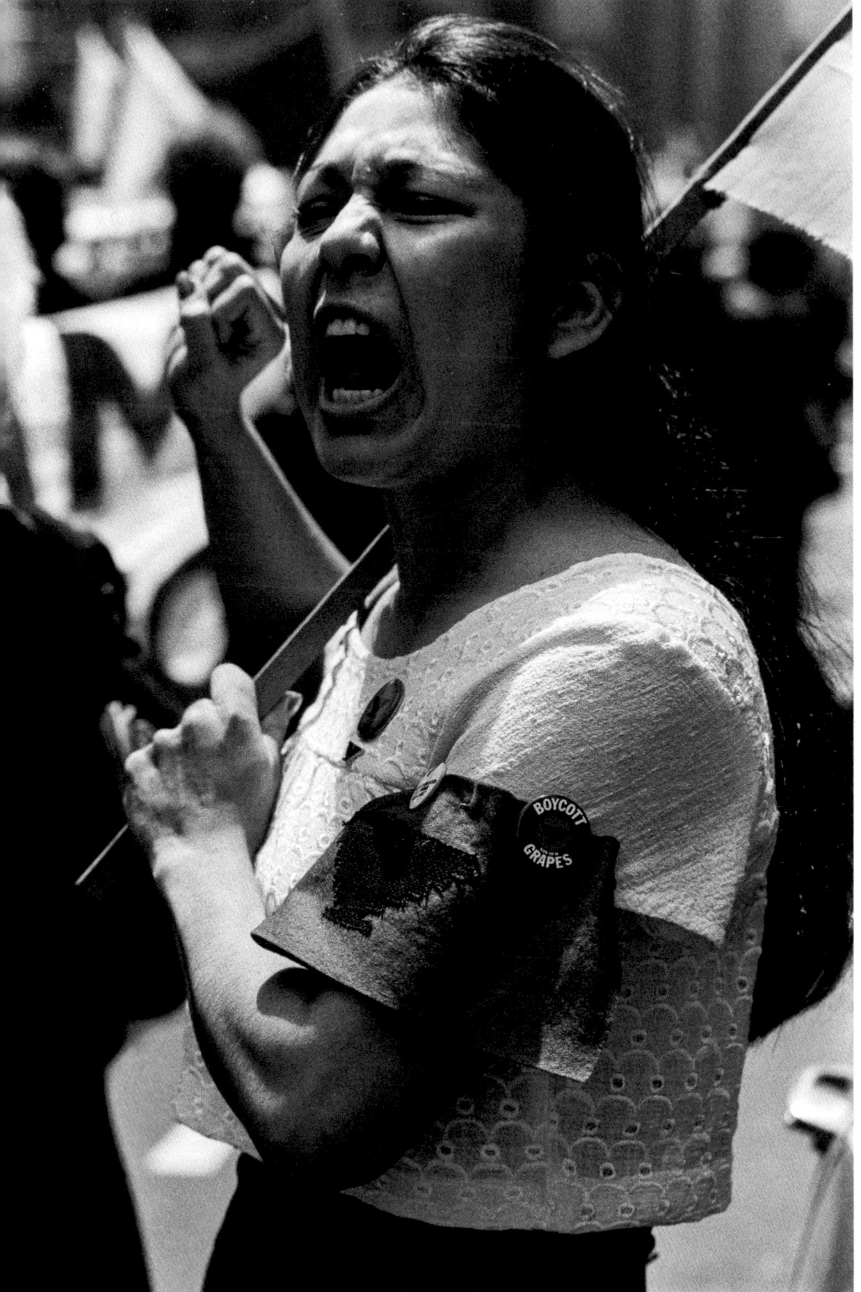

BOYCOTT
GRAPES

51. Worker laying underground power lines, New York, ca. 1972–1974.

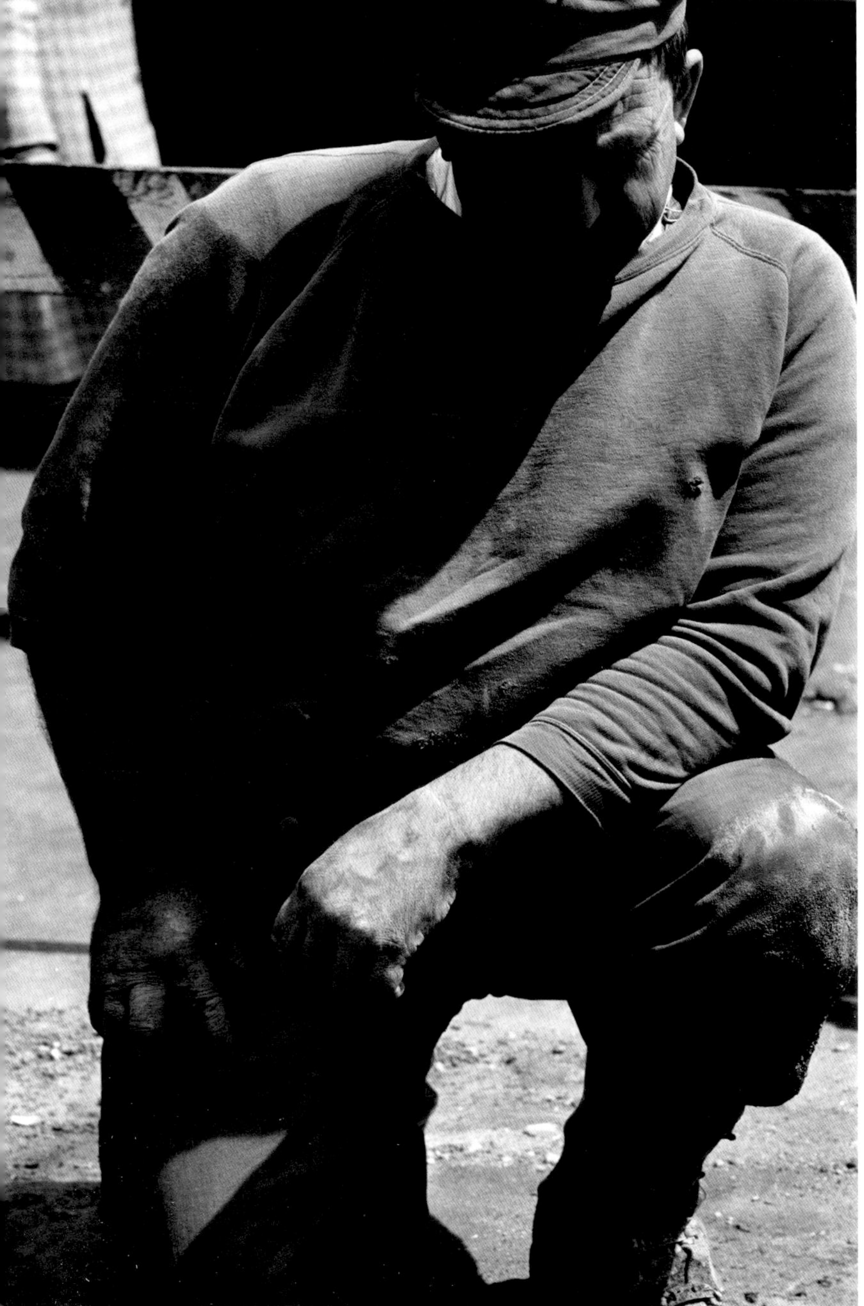

52. Pneumatic drill operator, Broadway, New York, ca. 1972–1974.

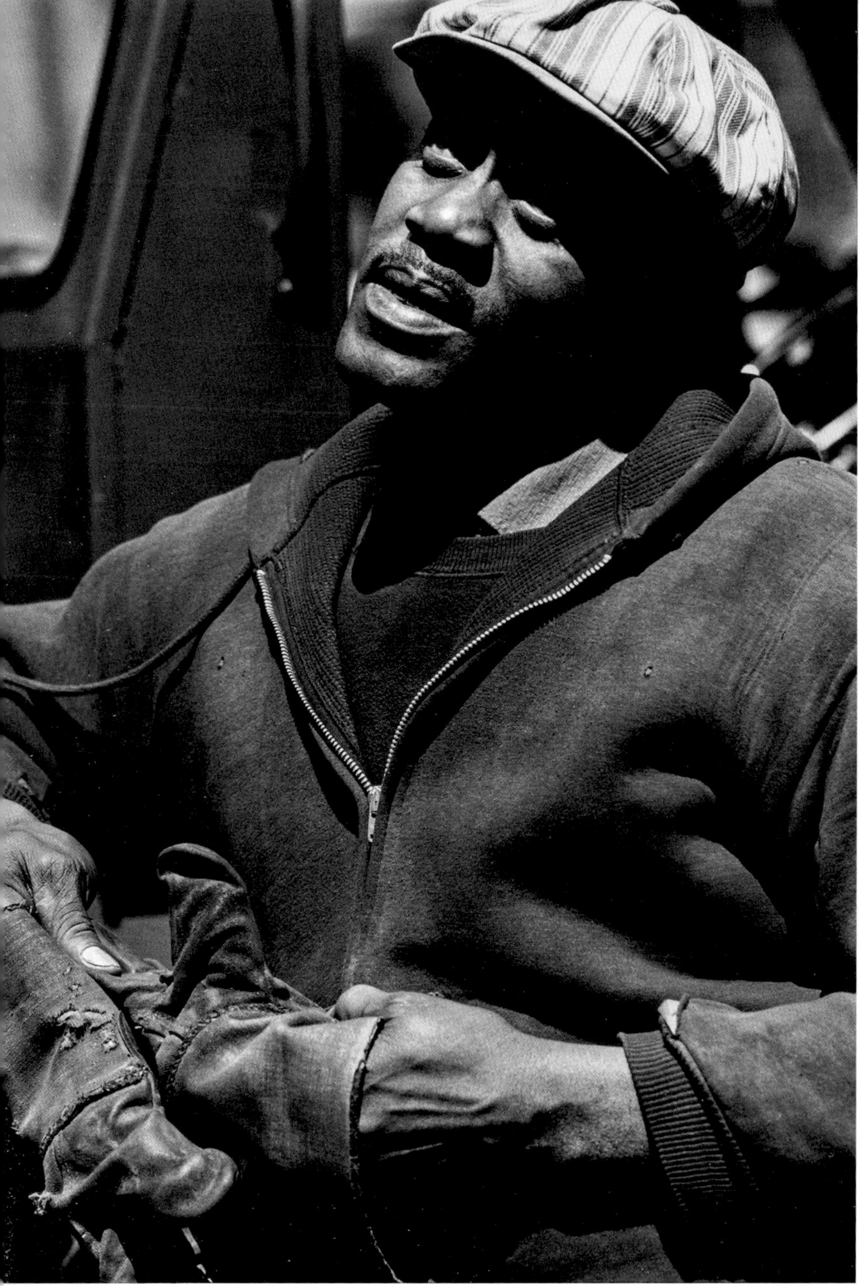

53. Nighttime, man sleeping, New York, ca. 2002–2005.

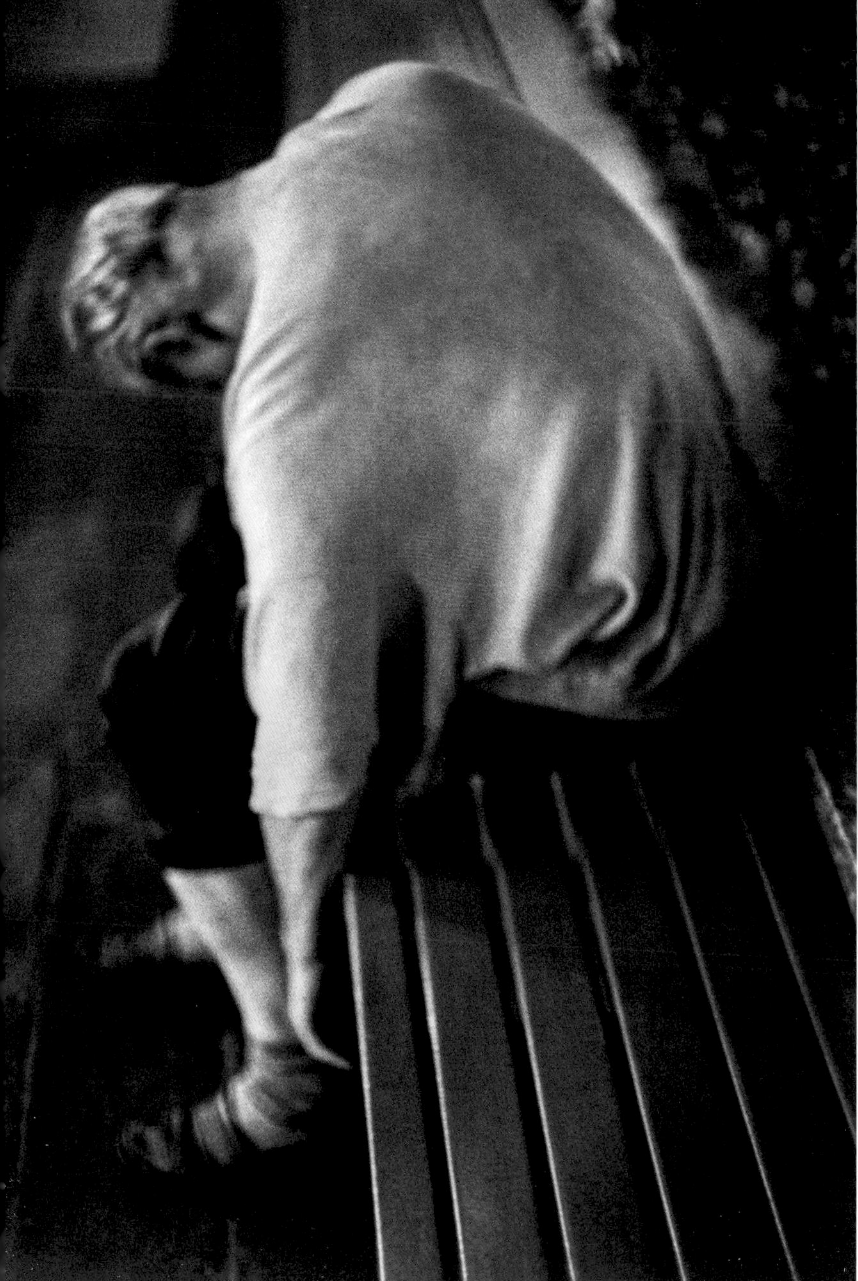

54. Women from Texas, Fifth Avenue, New York, ca. 1975.

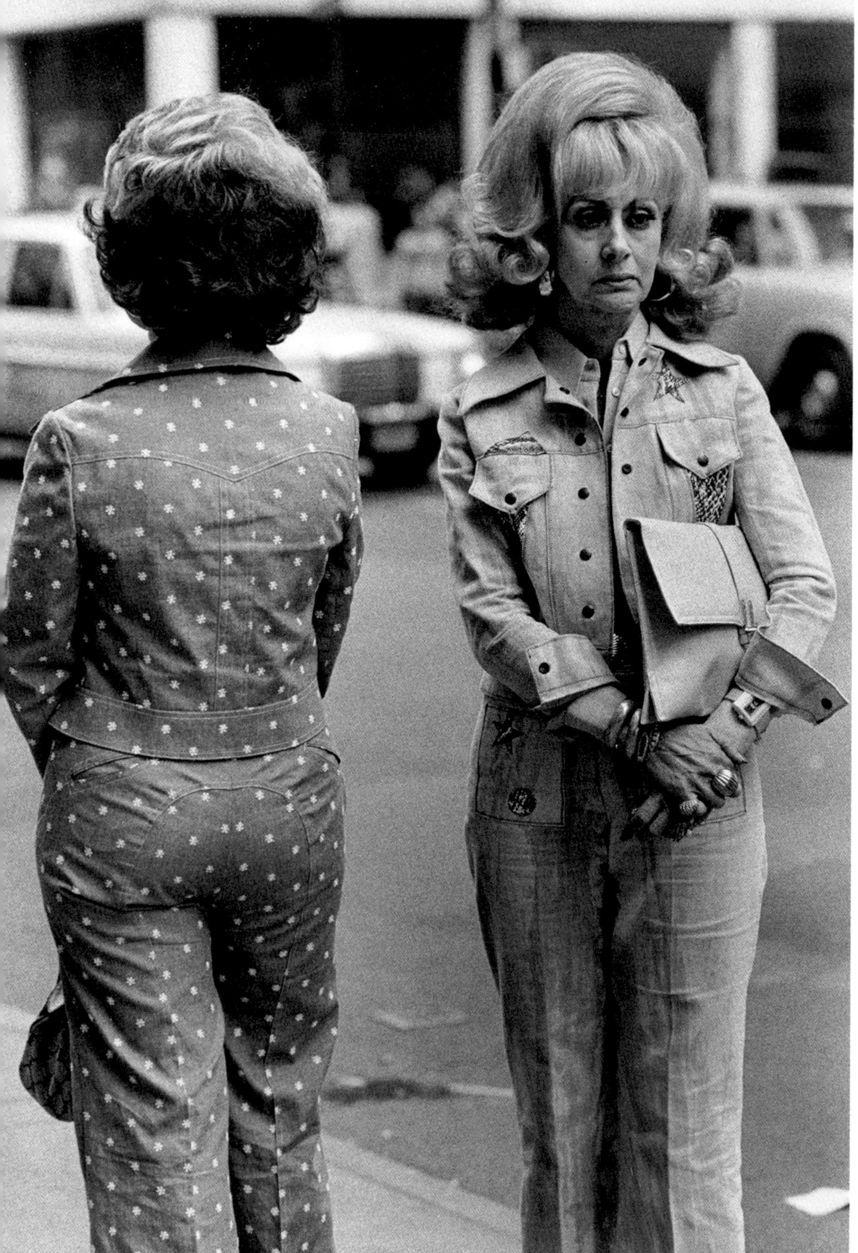

55. Police officer, New York, 1970s.

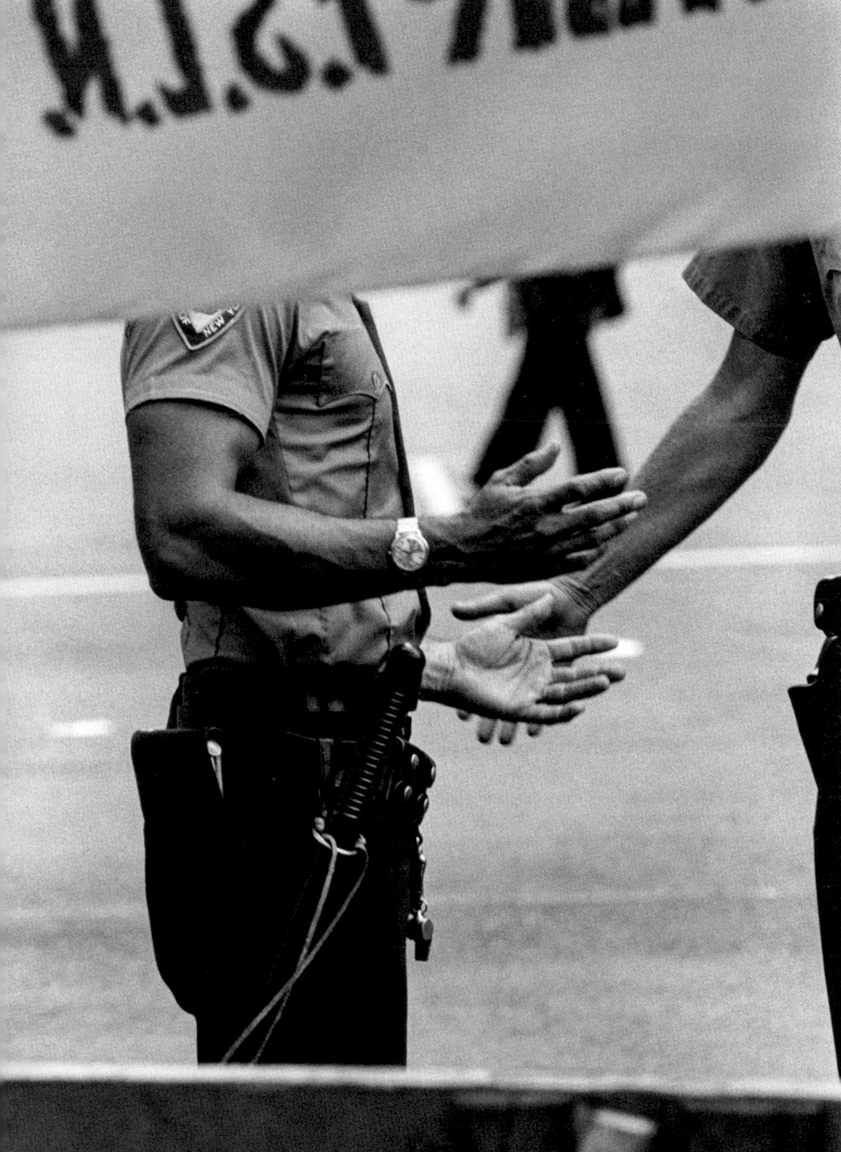

56. Near Canal Street, New York, ca. 1985.

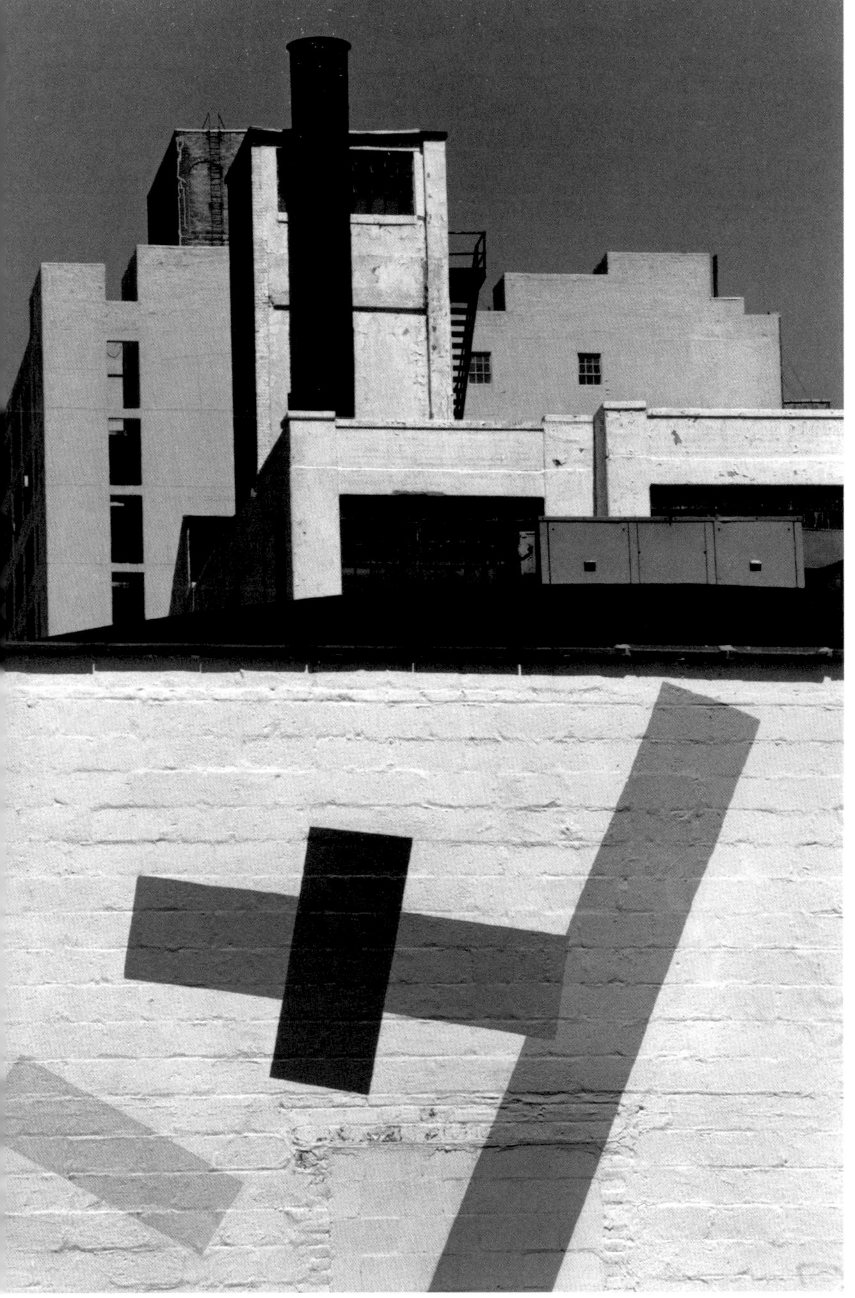

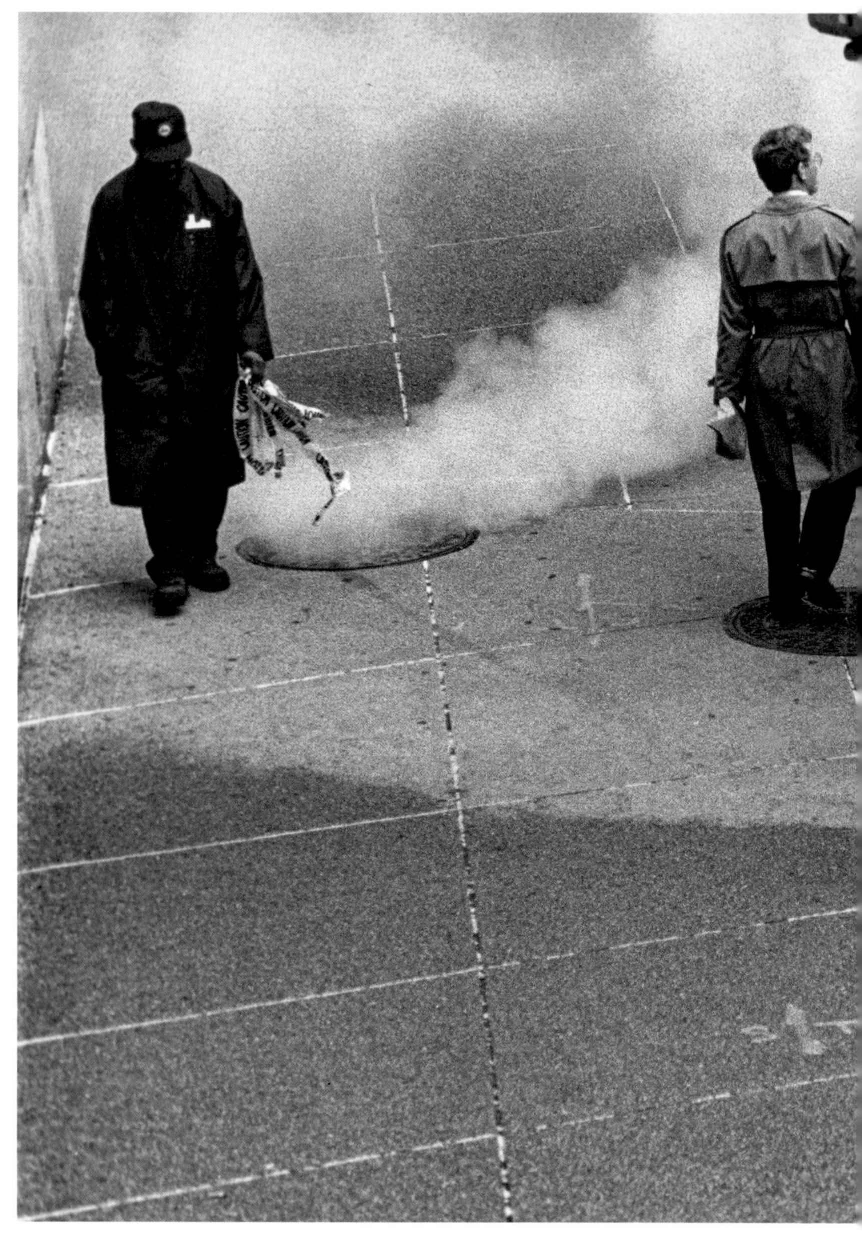

57. Near the World Trade Center, New York, ca. 1998.

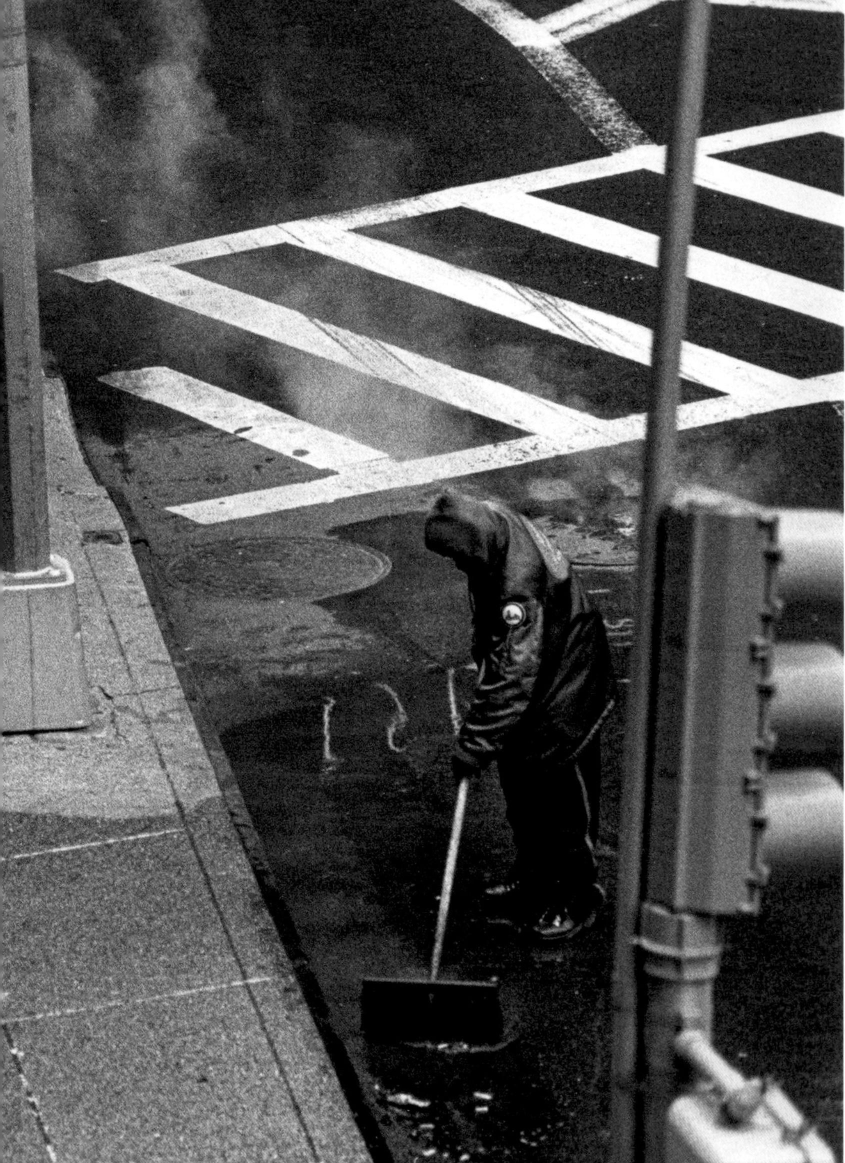

58. Fifth Avenue, New York, ca. 1976.

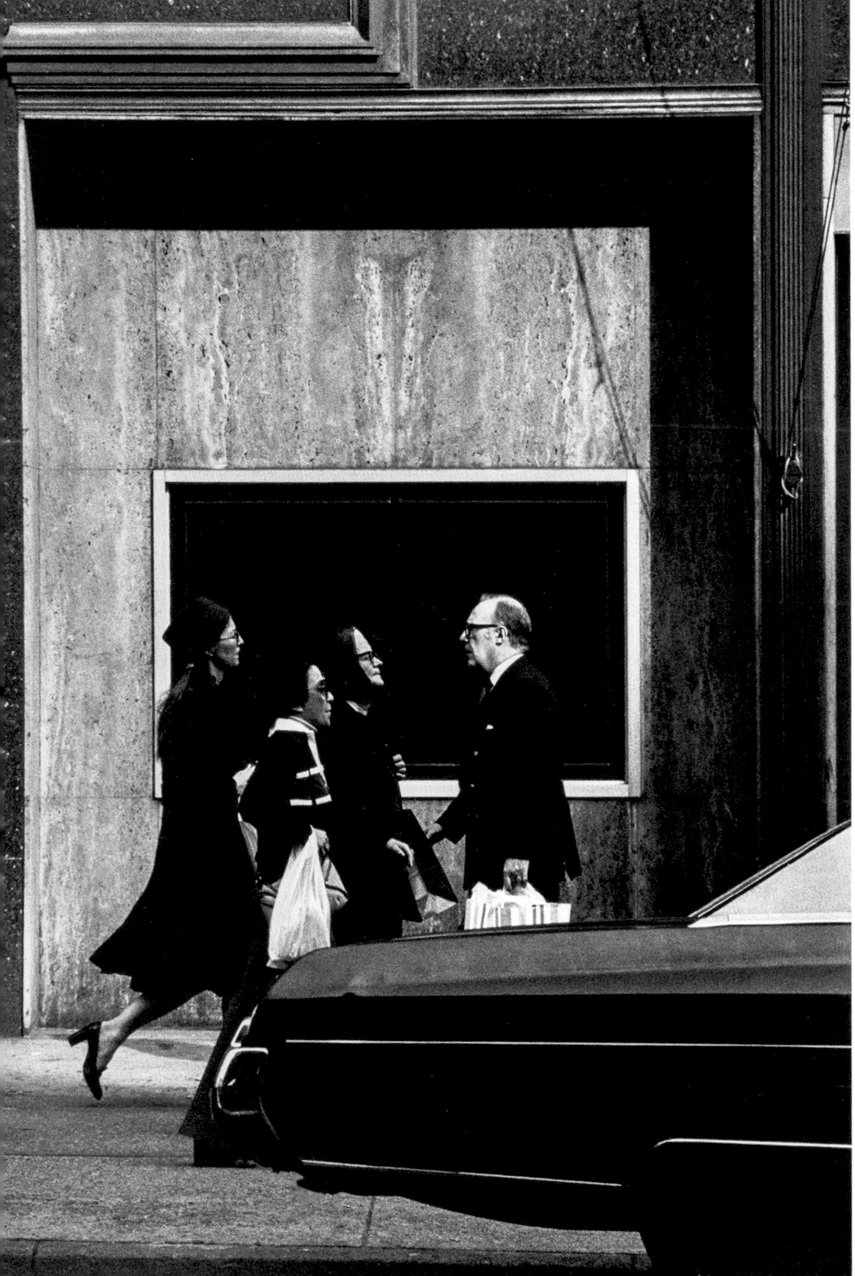

59. New York, 1970s.

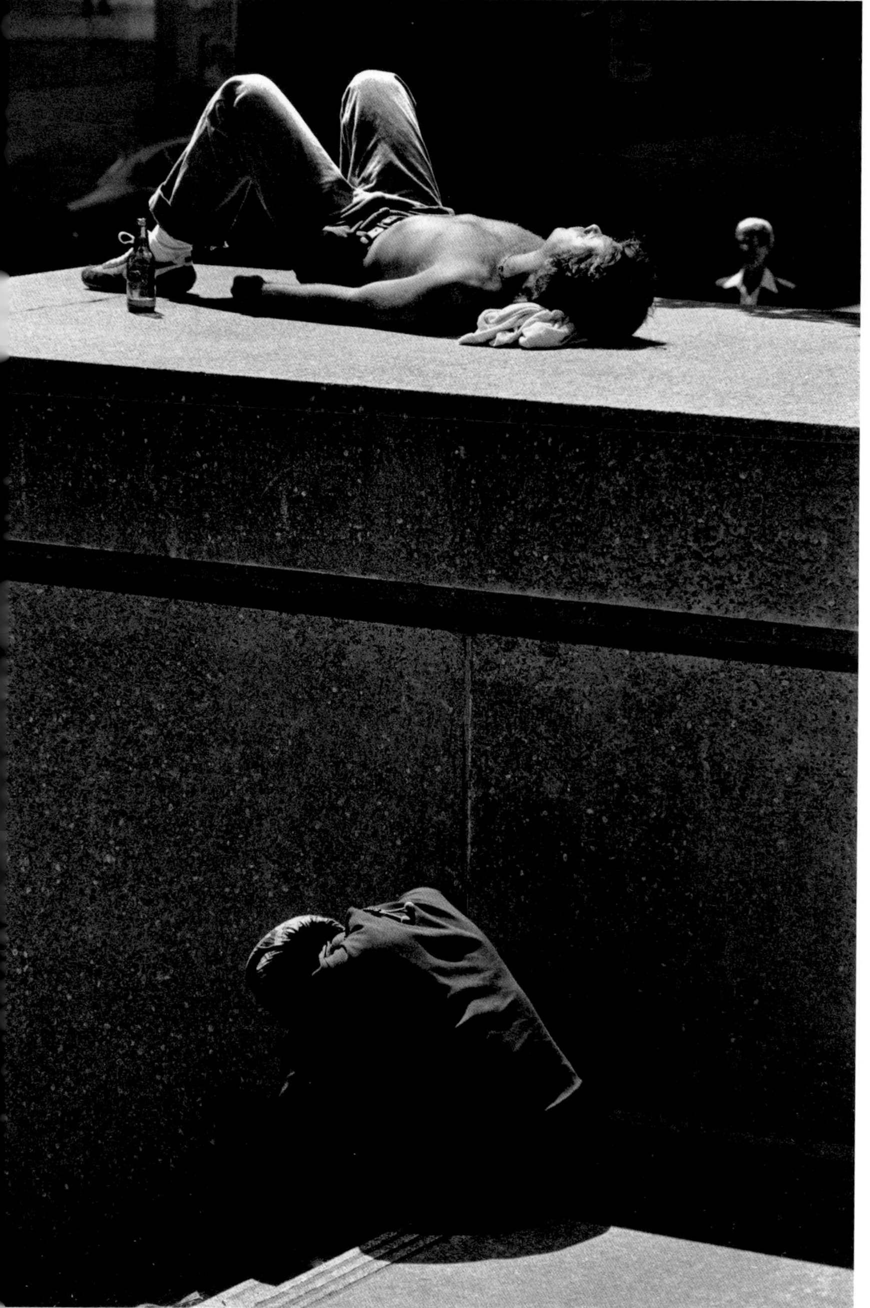

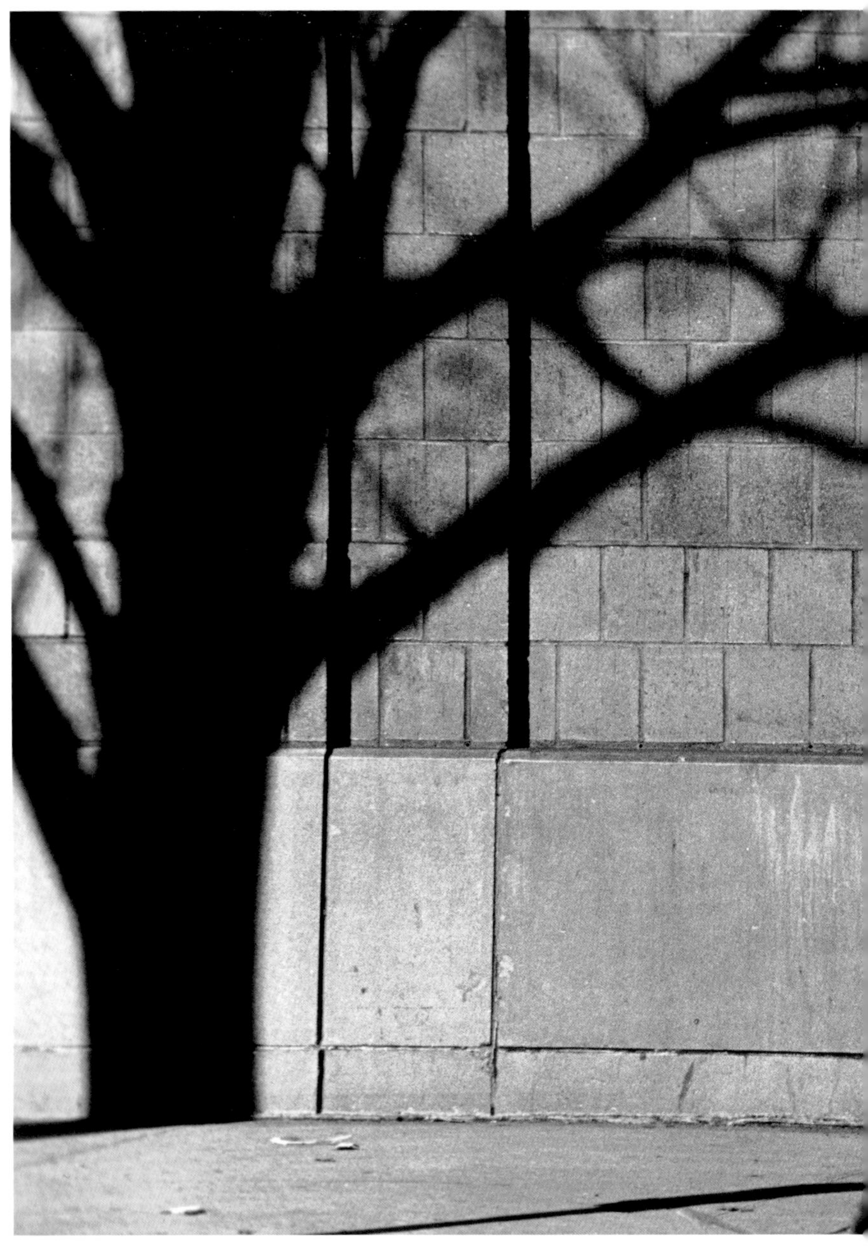

60. New York, ca. 2002.

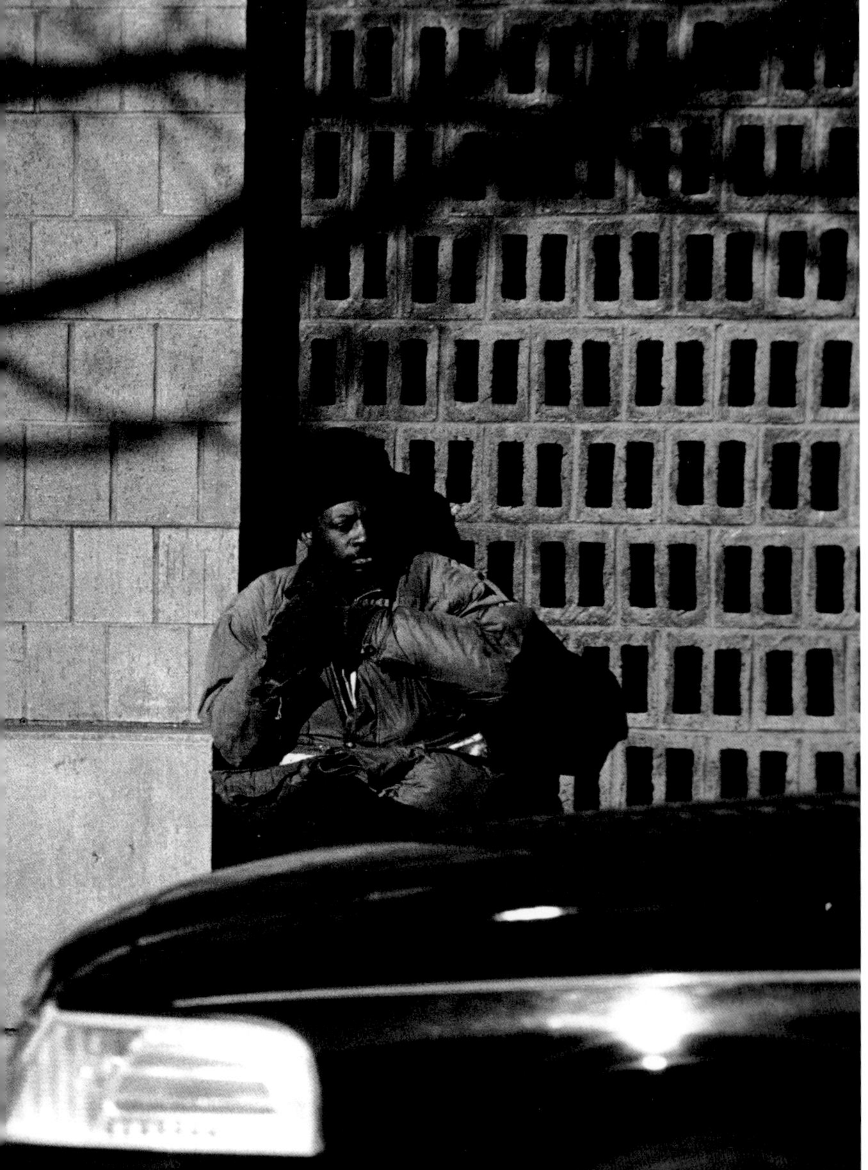

61. Janet, Florida, ca. 1982.

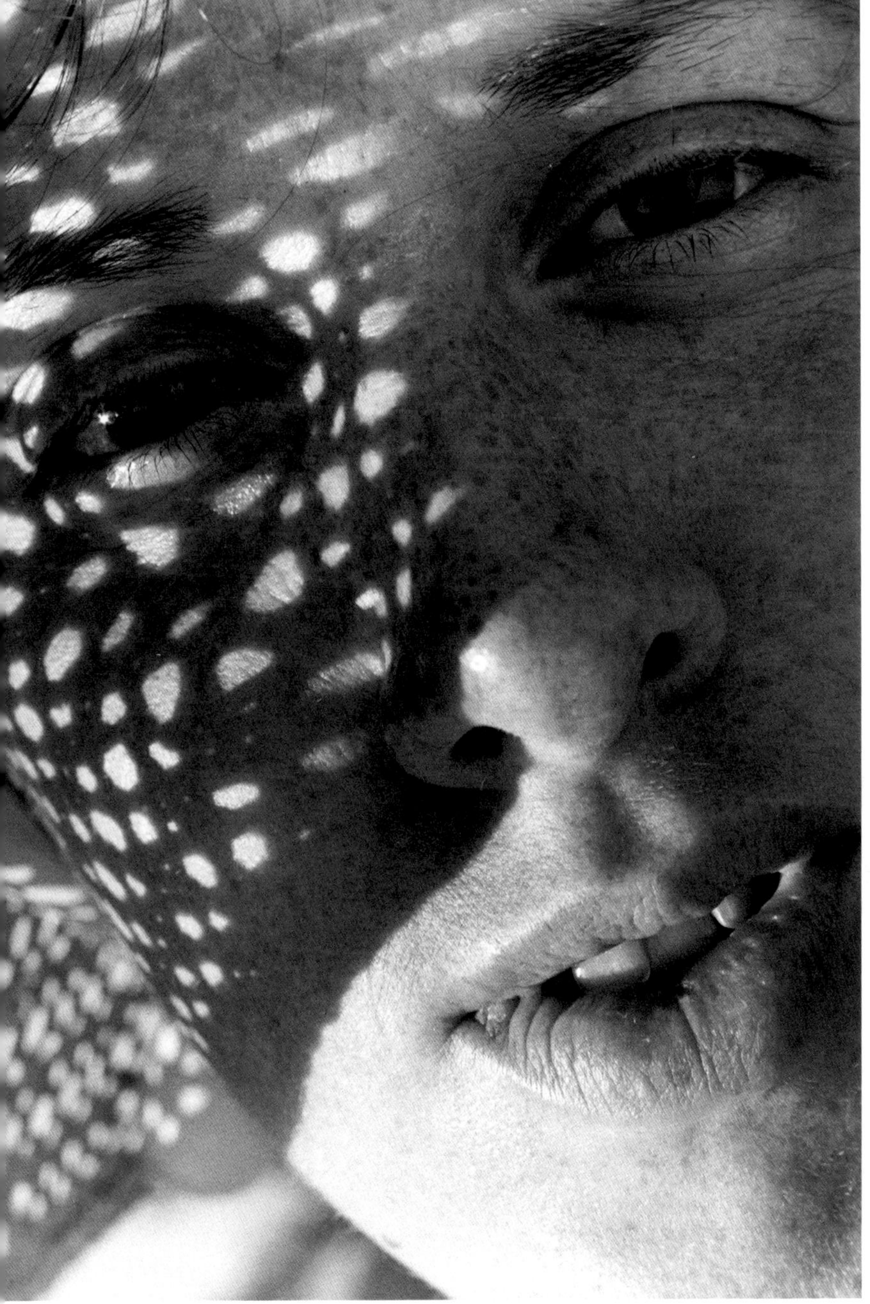

62. Janet, Athens, New York, 1988.

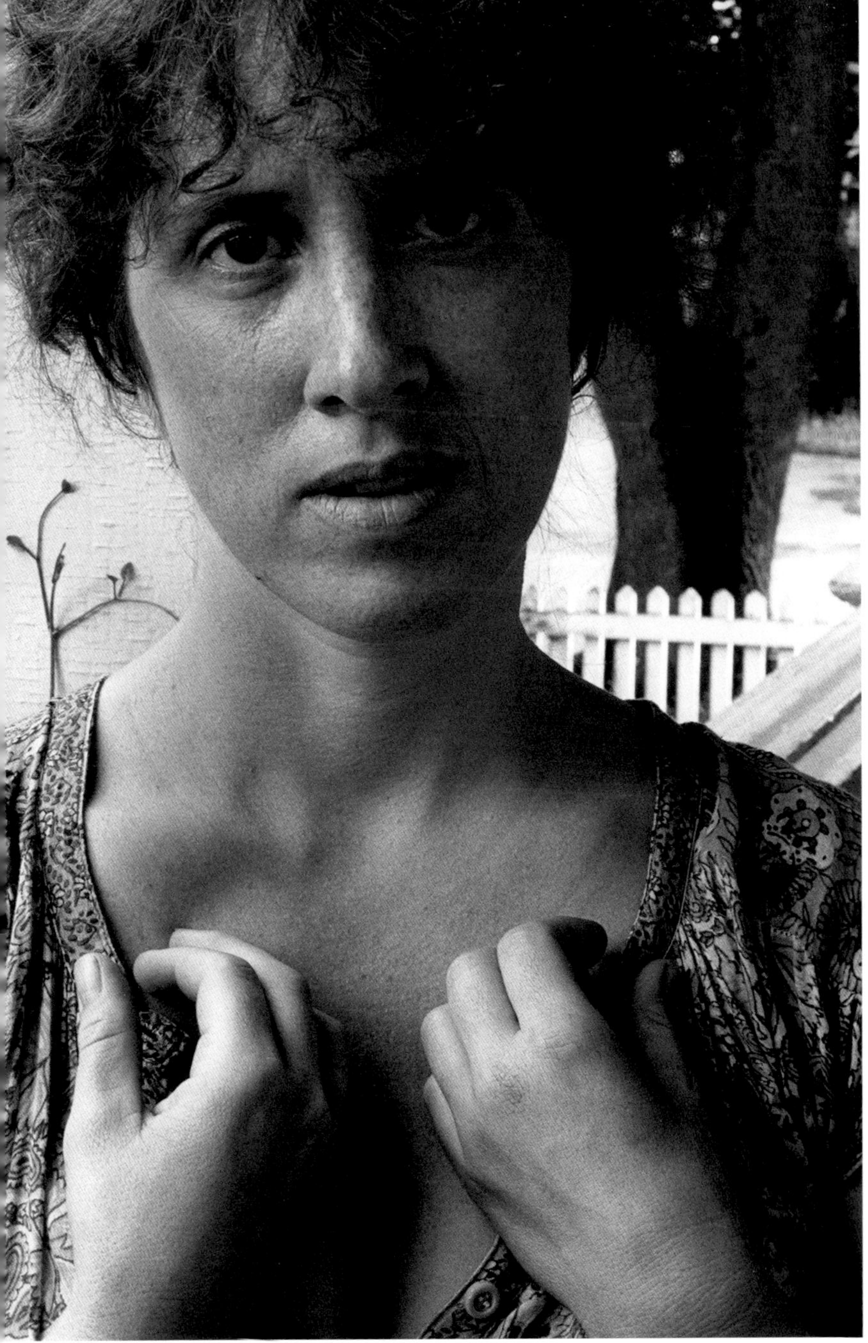

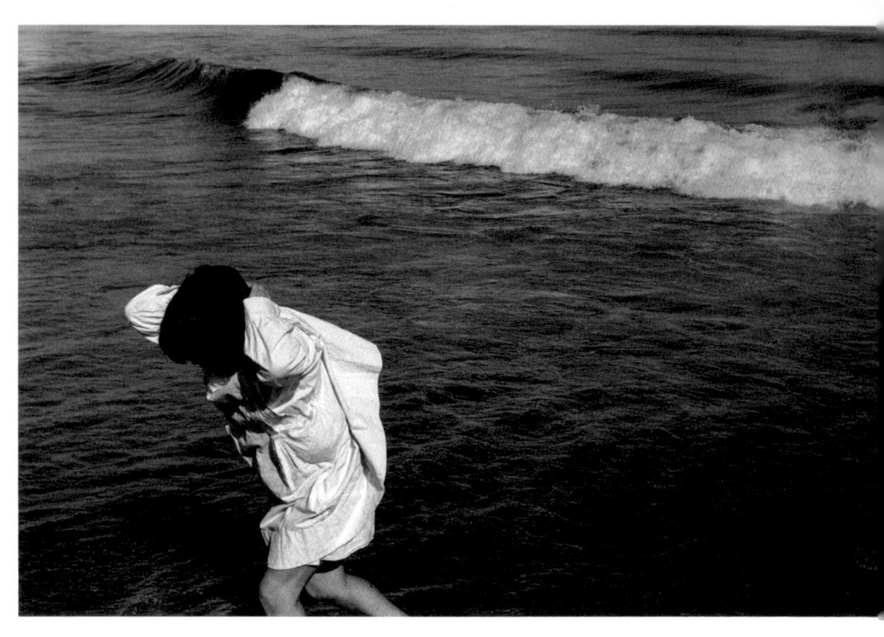

63. Girl in the sea, Spain, ca. 1959.
64. Wyoming, ca. 1977.

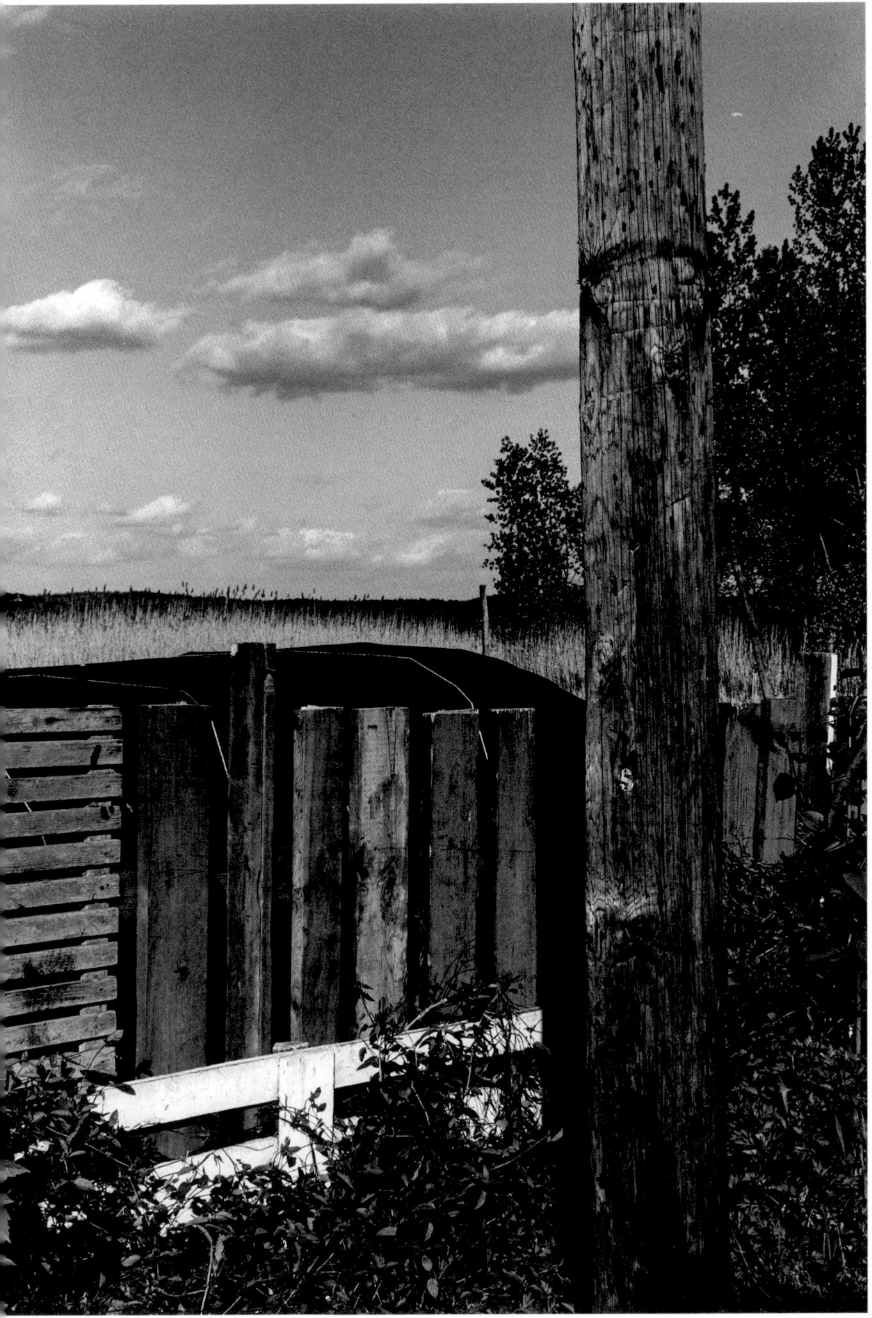

65. Montana, ca. 1977.

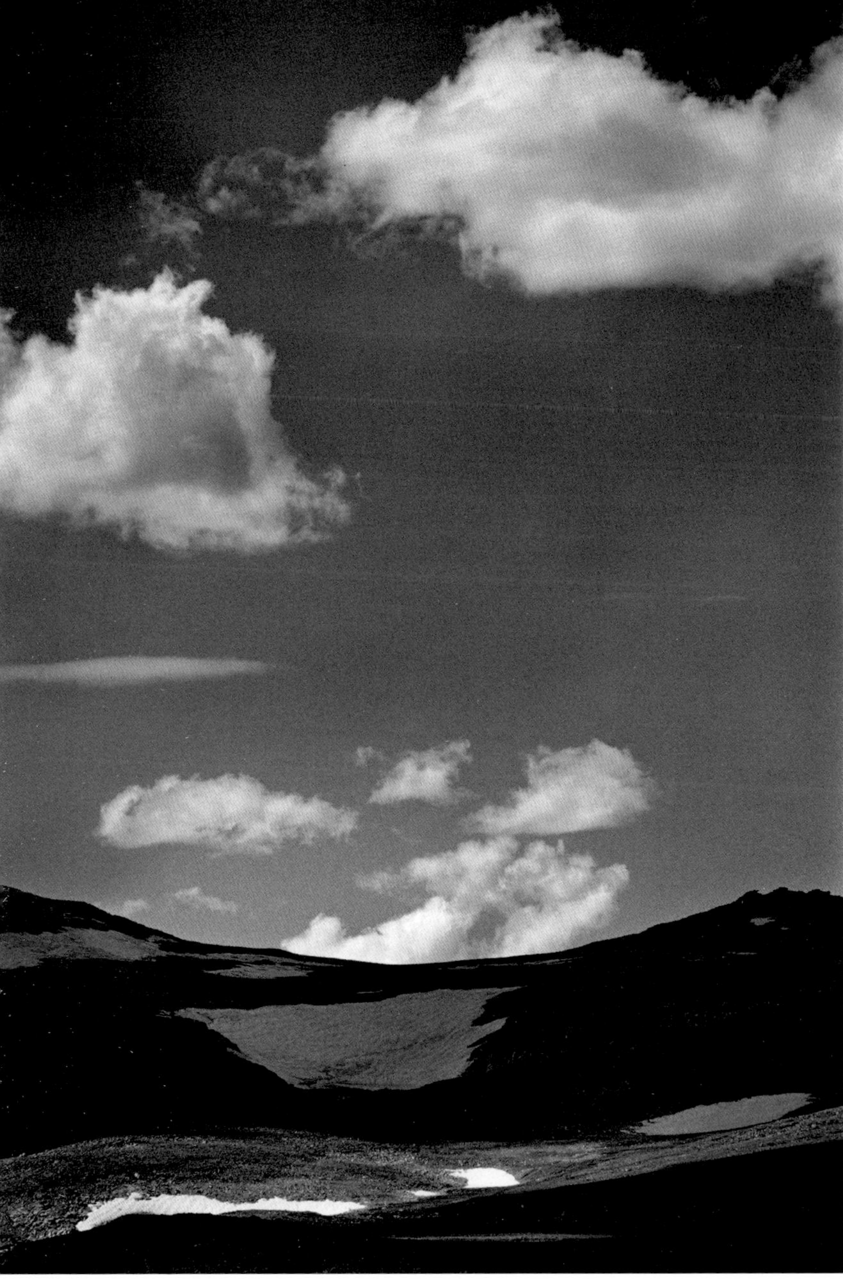

66. Montana, ca. 1977.

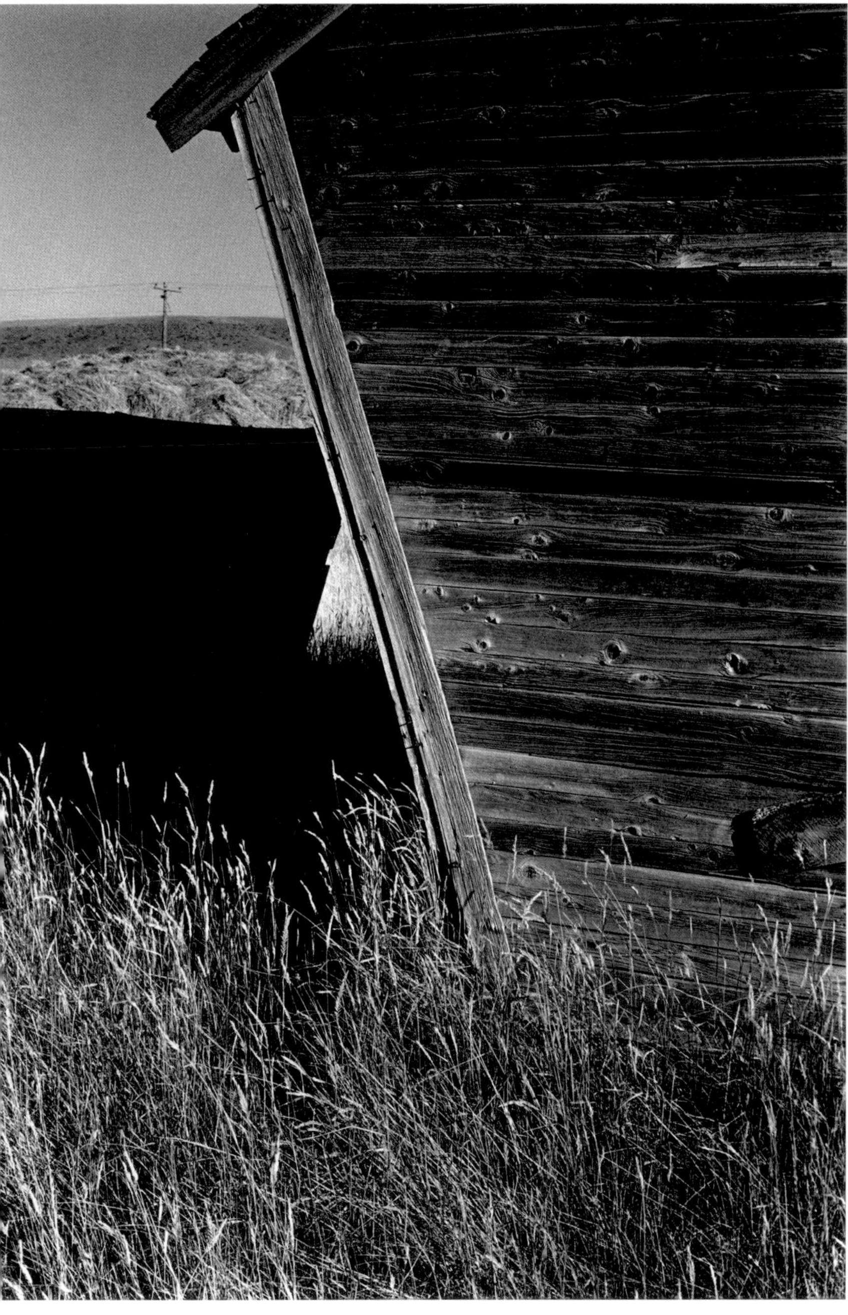

67. Les Alpilles, 2013.

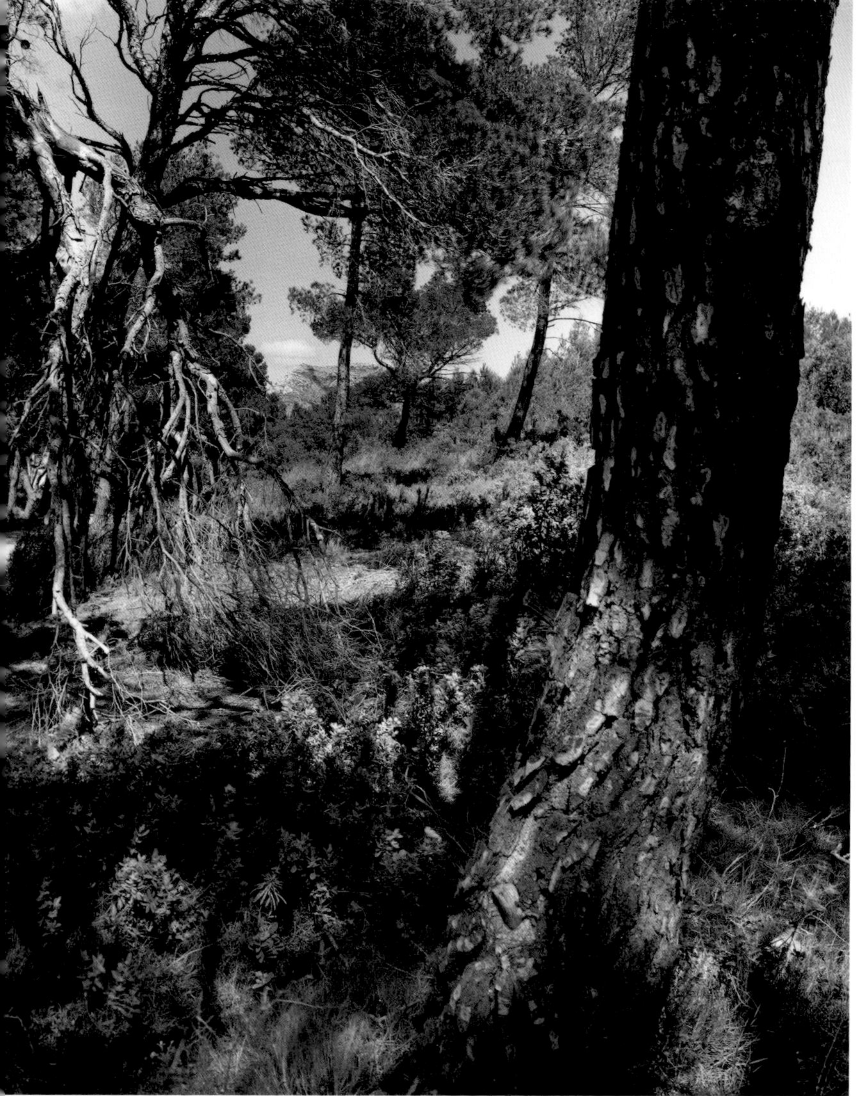

Biography

1922 Louis Stettner is born on November 7 in Brooklyn, New York, to Jewish parents originally from Czernowitz in Austria-Hungary. He has two older brothers, David and Max, and an identical twin, Irving.

1930s Takes a sculpture class and discovers African art.

1935–1942 Takes up amateur photography and becomes interested in the history of photography. Looks at original prints by master photographers at the Metropolitan Museum of Art, buys back issues of *Camera Work* magazine, regularly visits Alfred Stieglitz's gallery An American Place, meets Paul Strand, and attends a class taught by Max Drucker at the Photo League school.

1942–1945 Joins the U.S. Army as a photographer. After training in Arkansas, Princeton and Long Island, he is sent to the front lines in New Guinea and the Philippines. Photographs the ruins of Hiroshima three weeks after its destruction by atomic bomb.

1946 Shoots a series of photographs in the New York subway, which is published a year later in the arts and literature review *The New Iconograph*, accompanied by a text by photographer Sid Grossman.

1947 Teaches photographic technique at the Photo League school. He contacts Willy Ronis and leaves for Paris in July, planning to organize an exhibition of French photography at the Photo League's gallery in New York. In December 1947, the Photo League is placed on the blacklist of subversive organizations.

1947–1952 Lives in Paris and travels throughout Europe. He befriends Brassaï, Paul Strand, Édouard Boubat, Rune Hassner, Tore Johnson, William Eugene Smith and Robert Frank. Studies filmmaking at the Institut des Hautes Études Cinématographiques (IDHEC) thanks to the G.I. Bill and makes two short films. Is commissioned by the Economic Cooperation Administration, the government agency overseeing the Marshall Plan, to take photographs in France and Norway, but loses the job due to his links with the Photo League.

1948 An exhibition of twelve French photographers, selected by Louis Stettner, opens at the Photo League's gallery in New York. Accompanied by a text by photography historian Beaumont Newhall, this is the first time Robert Doisneau, Édouard Boubat, and Willy Ronis are exhibited in the U.S.

1952–1959 Settles first in the East Village and then on Seventh Avenue, New York. He works for the press and advertising, while continuing to shoot his own photographs.

1956 Visits Mexico. Attends a residency at Yaddo artist's colony in Saratoga Springs, New York, where he meets the writer Saul Bellow.

1958 Produces the record *Famous Photographers Tell How*, featuring interviews with Henri Cartier-Bresson, Weegee, Philippe Halsman, Arthur Rothstein and Bert Stern.

1959–1964 Extended sojourns in France, Portugal, the UK, Spain, Greece, and the Netherlands, where he works for magazines and advertising agencies. Writes novels, short stories, and plays.

1961 Has a daughter, Isobel Charlotte, with Betty Julia Ensel.

1965 Returns to New York and lives on Manhattan's Upper West Side.

1966 Has a son, Patrick Samuel, with Christine Gabrielle Rollet.

ca. 1968 Takes up sculpture again and becomes interested in Art Brut, as promoted by Jean Dubuffet.

1969–1977 Placed under FBI surveillance due to his links with the Communist Party USA.

1971–1979 Writes a column for the magazine *Camera 35*, at first entitled *Speaking Out*, then renamed *A Humanist View*.

1972–1975 Photographs *Workers*, a series on factory workers, for which he receives a National Endowment for the Arts.

1973–1977 Teaches at Brooklyn College of the City University of New York, Cooper Union for the Advancement of Science and Art, and in the Art Department of the C.W. Post Center at Long Island University.

1975 Wins a competition run by the Soviet
newspaper *Pravda* and travels to the USSR
for a month.

1981 Marries Janet Martha Iffland.

1981–1990 Focuses on his own photography,
shooting several series: *Nudes*, *Manhattan
Trilogy*, *Manhattan Walls* and *Pavement*.

1982 Janet and Louis acquire a house in
Athens, New York, a small town on the
Hudson River. Their son Anton is born.

1986 Their son Arion is born.

1988 The Centre Pompidou stages a show
at the Galerie du Forum, recreating the
exhibition of French photography originally
organized by Louis Stettner in New York in
1948, which was rediscovered and acquired
forty years later by the Musée National d'Art
Moderne.

1990 His brother David Stettner dies. Louis
and Janet buy a house in Saint-Ouen from
Michel and Michèle Auer, and move there
permanently, although they continue to
visit Manhattan and Athens, New York
for vacations.

1990 Begins a series of collages called *Marché
aux Puces*. Begins to paint, in parallel with
his sculpture work. Continues to shoot his
own photographs in New York and Paris,
occasionally returning to the square format.

2000 Awarded the title of Chevalier des Arts
et des Lettres in France.

2000–2010 Photographs the series *Manhattan
Pastorale* and *New York Color*, printed in
Cibachrome by Roland Dufau. Also shoots
personal projects in black and white in
New York, Athens, Paris, and Chile.

2013–2016 Visits the French region of Les
Alpilles thirteen times to shoot a series on
trees with a large-format view camera.

2016 Louis Stettner dies in Paris on October 13.

Selected Bibliography

Monographs

10 Photographs by Louis Stettner, introduction by Brassaï, Paris & New York: Two Cities Publications, 1949

U.S. Camera's 35 mm Photography, New York: U.S. Camera Publishing Corp., 1956

History of the Nude in American Photography, Greenwich, CT: Whitestones, 1966

Workers, text by Howard Greenberg and Jacob Deschin, New York: Stettner Studio, 1974

Women, New York: Stettner Studio, 1975

Weegee, New York: Alfred A. Knopf; Toronto: Random House of Canada, 1977

Sur le tas. Portraits d'hommes et de femmes au travail, text by François Cavanna, Paris: Éditions du Cercle d'Art, 1979

Early Joys, text by Brassaï, New York: Janet Iffland Publisher, 1987

Sous le ciel de Paris, text by François Cavanna, Paris: Parigramme, 1994

Louis Stettner's New York 1950s–1990s, text by Barbara Einzig, New York: Rizzoli, 1996

Louis Stettner: American Photographer, Aix-la-Chapelle: Suermondt-Ludwig-Museum, 1996

Louis Stettner: Photo Poche, text by François Bernheim, Paris: Nathan, 1998

Louis Stettner. Sophisme. Photographies 1990–1999, interview with Michèle Auer, Neuchâtel: Ides et Calendes, "Photogalerie," 1999

Wisdom Cries Out in the Streets, Paris: Flammarion, 1999

Louis Stettner. Photographie peinture sculpture, Paris: Éditions Casta Diva, 2009

Louis Stettner photographe, Éditions Casta Diva, Paris: 2012

Louis Stettner: Penn Station, New York, text by Adam Gopnik, New York: Thames & Hudson, 2015

Louis Stettner. Ici ailleurs, eds. Clément Chéroux and Julie Jones, Paris: Éditions du Centre Pompidou/Éditions Xavier Barral, 2016

Louis Stettner: Traveling Light, text by Clément Chéroux and Sally Martin Katz, Paris: Cernunnos, 2019

Louis Stettner, ed. Sally Martin Katz, Madrid: Fundación MAPFRE, 2023; London: Thames & Hudson, 2024

Other publications

Louis Stettner, "An evening in an important asylum," *First Stage*, vol. 6, no. 2, summer, Purdue University, Lafayette, IN, 1967

Weegee Portfolio, 45 gelatin silver prints by Sid Kaplan, text by Louis Stettner, New York: The Weegee Collection, 1986

Laure Beaumont-Maillet, Françoise Denoyelle and Dominique Versavel (eds.), *La Photographie humaniste, 1945–1968. Autour d'Izis, Boubat, Brassaï, Doisneau, Ronis...*, Paris: Bibliothèque Nationale de France, 2006

Mason Klein and Catherine Evans (eds.), *The Radical Camera: New York's Photo League 1936–1951*, New Haven, CT: Yale University Press, 2012

Selected Exhibitions

Solo exhibitions

1954 "Louis Stettner," Limelight Gallery, New York.

1958 "Small Town—Big Town," E. Leitz Gallery, New York.

1959 Louis Stettner, Bennos Foto, Stockholm.

1964 "Europe 2," Village Camera Club, New York.

1971 "Louis Stettner," George Eastman House, Rochester, NY.

1973 "Louis Stettner," Witkin Gallery, New York.

1974 "The Workers Portfolio," Neikrug Gallery, New York.

1976 "Louis Stettner Photographs," Gallery 1199, New York.

1983 "Louis Stettner," Addison Gallery of American Art, Phillips Academy, Andover, MA. "Recent Photographs," Midtown Y Photography Gallery, New York.

1986 "Photographies 1949–1985," Centre de la Photographie, Geneva.

1988 "Early Joys," Photofind Gallery, New York. "The Manhattan Trilogy," Union Square Gallery, New York.

1989 "Louis Stettner," Comptoir de la Photographie, Paris.

1990 "Retrospectiva 1945–1990," Iglesia de San Atilano, Tarazona, Spain. "Louis Stettner," Kate Hellner Gallery, London.

1992 "Love Notes from Paris: Recent Montages, Photographs, and Portfolios," Howard Greenberg Gallery, New York.

1996 "Train of Thought," Bonni Benrubi Gallery, New York.

1997 "Louis Stettner: American Photographer," Suermondt-Ludwig Museum, Aix-la-Chapelle.

2000 "Paintings," Galerie Marion Meyer, Paris. "Louis Stettner's Paris," Galerie Marion Meyer, Paris.

2001 "Chile en el corazón," Museo Nacional de Bellas Artes, Santiago de Chile.

2003 "Unseen Stettner 1946–2002," Bonni Benrubi Gallery, New York.

2004–2005 "Louis Stettner: Today and Yesterday," Galerie Esther Woerdehoff, Paris.

2006 "Louis Stettner: Photographien," Camera Work Gallery, Berlin.

2009 "Louis Stettner. New York / Paris," Base Sous-marine, Bordeaux.

2010 "Louis Stettner. Sophisme. Photographies 1990–1999," Château de Nyon, Switzerland.

2012 "Louis Stettner. Les chefs-d'oeuvre," Galerie David Guiraud, Paris.

2012–2013 "Louis Stettner photographe. Une rétrospective," Bibliothèque Nationale de France, Paris.

2015 "Louis Stettner, 40 ans d'amitié Paris New York," Fondation Auer Ory pour la Photographie, Hermance, Switzerland.

2016 "Louis Stettner. Ici ailleurs," Centre Pompidou, Paris. "Louis Stettner," Galerie Susse Frères, Paris.

2018 "Manhattan Pastorale," Tibor de Nagy Gallery, New York.

2018–2019 "Traveling Light," San Francisco Museum of Modern Art.

2019 "A Day to Remember," Gallery Fifty One, Antwerp.

2022 "The Last Word," The Hulett Collection, Tulsa, OK.

2023–2025 "Louis Stettner," Fundación MAPFRE, Madrid; KBr Fundación MAPFRE – Barcelona Photo Center, Barcelona; Centro Andaluz de la Fotografía, Almería.

2023–2024 "Chromatic Reverie," The Hulett Collection, Tulsa, OK.

2025 "Le Monde de Louis Stettner (1922–2016)," Espace Van Gogh, Rencontres Internationales de la Photographie, Arles.

Group exhibitions

1950 "Cinquième Salon de la Photographie," Bibliothèque Nationale de France, Paris.

1951 "Subjektive Fotografie," Staatliche Schule für Kunst und Handwerk, Saarbrücken.

1975 "Photographers Forum Exhibition," Brooklyn Museum, New York.

1978 "Photographic Crossroads: The Photo

League," National Gallery of Canada, Ottawa; Minneapolis Institute of Arts.

1980 "Brad Temkin, Louis Stettner," Milwaukee Center for Photography.

1986 "City Light," International Center of Photography, New York.

1990 "Chefs-d'oeuvre de la photographie, les années 1950," Fondation Select, Salon du Livre et de la Presse, Geneva.

1994 "84–94," Centre de la Photographie, Geneva; Fondazione Galleria Gottardo, Lugano.

1997 "De quelques sculptures...," Galerie Marion Meyer, Paris.

1998 "Flashback: The Fifties," Bonni Benrubi Gallery, New York.

1999 "Photo League," Espacio Fundación Telefónica, PHotoESPAÑA, Madrid.

2011–2013 "The Radical Camera: New York's Photo League 1936–1951," The Jewish Museum, New York; Columbus Museum of Art, OH; The Contemporary Jewish Museum, San Francisco; Norton Museum of Art, West Palm Beach, FL.

2015 "New York," Les Douches la Galerie, Paris.

2022–2023 "Centennial: Saul Leiter, Jan Yoors, Louis Stettner," Gallery Fifty One, Antwerp.

2023–2024 "Corps à corps. Histoire(s) de la photographie," Centre Pompidou, Paris. "Noir & blanc. Une esthétique de la photographie," Bibliothèque Nationale de France, Paris.

2024 "Présences. Trésors photographiques de la collection Gilman et Gonzalez-Falla," Maison Caillebotte, Yerres.

Other productions

1958 Louis Stettner (prod.), *Famous Photographers Tell How*, Candid Recordings, New York, audio recording.

1999 Christophe Debuisne, *Au regard de la mémoire de Louis Stettner*, Modom Productions, 23:30 mins, film.

The Photofile series is the original English-language edition of the Photo Poche collection. It was first published between 1986 and 1992 by the Centre National de la Photographie, Paris, with the support of the French Ministry of Culture. Robert Delpire (1926–2017) was the creator of the series and its managing editor until 2017.

Series design by Matthew Young

General editor: Géraldine Lay

First published in the United Kingdom in 2025 by
Thames & Hudson Ltd, 6–24 Britannia Street, London WC1X 9JD

First published in 2025 in the United States of America by
Thames & Hudson Inc., 500 Fifth Avenue, New York, New York 10110

Photo Poche © 2025 Actes Sud, France
Photographs by Louis Stettner © Archives Louis Stettner, Saint-Ouen
This edition © 2025 Thames & Hudson Ltd, London

EU Authorized Representative: Interart S.A.R.L.
19 rue Charles Auray, 93500 Pantin, Paris, France
productsafety@thameshudson.co.uk
www.interart.fr

A CIP catalogue record for this book is available from the British Library

Library of Congress Catalog Card Number 2025934130

ISBN 978-0-500-41132-2
01

Printed and bound in Italy